LAND'S END TO JOHN O'GROATS

Sean Conway

Land's End to John O'Groats

Published by Mortimer Lion Publishing
First published in 2012

ISBN: 978-0-9574497-3-2

www.SeanConway.com
Twitter: Conway_Sean

For
Andrew 'Cad' Cadigan

Introduction

Thank you for buying my first proper non-fiction adventure novel. I have done everything from the editing, the proof reading, designing the cover, printing and publishing. That's probably not the most sensible thing to do, but it means if there is anything wrong with it, then I can't blame anyone else but myself. It's been a great experience and I have loved every step of it. This is going to be the first of many books I write about my adventures, both past and future.

To find out more about me, and my adventures go to **www.SeanConway.com**

Yours in adventure,

Sean Conway

Contents

Why?

So it was holiday booking time again and as usual I was looking at flights to all the exotic parts of the world like Thailand, The Maldives and The Seychelles. I then remembered I wasn't related to Richard Branson, and was forced to look into holidays a little closer to home.

Looking for a holiday has always been tough for me. Being of the ginger variety meant that beach holidays orientated around a sun bed weren't an option for my vampire complexion. I may as well spend a week in a microwave on full power. I was looking for something adventurous, fun and on this occasion in particular, a little physically challenging.

I then spent another week pretending Sir Richard was my personal bank account while looking into Polar Expeditions, Everest Summits and Atlantic Rows. It was pointless. I couldn't afford any of them. (Damn you, Richard. Please reply to my letters so we can be friends...)

Pretty depressed by the whole situation I gave in and found a package holiday to skin-cancer-ville and was literally clicking on the checkout button when my flatmate asked me whether I'd been to The Lake District. No, was my answer. What about The Highlands? No! Devon? No! Peak District? No! And so it continued. "No, no, um, no but my train went through there once."

It was embarrassing. I had lived in the UK for nearly 6

years and hadn't even been to Wales, which I'm told was less than 3 hours drive away. That wasn't right and I was embarrassed at how little I knew about the country I lived in. With that, I shut down lastminute.com and decided I'd do something in Britain. This excited me a lot.

Another week went by thinking about all the various ways I could see Britain, like running, walking or skateboarding, (Don't laugh. My friend Dave has done that,) but the one that kept coming up was cycling the iconic Land's End to John O'Groats. I wasn't a cyclist but I figured if I took it slow enough I'd make it, eventually.

So with that logic my plan was set. I'd attempt to become the 7654679th person (I made that figure up, I have no idea how many people have done it) to cycle Land's End to John O'Groats.

I couldn't wait.

6

The day before

"3.... 2.... 1.... down, down, down."

I over-theatrically downed the double Sambuca and without even wincing, followed it with Apple Sours. That's not a great combination by the way – my friends are evil. Also, Apple Sours? I'm not 15 years old. Still holding both shot glasses, I traditionally tapped the table 3 times and gave a not so manly growl. Honestly. Who growls?

Everyone cheered and laughed, as they knew this was going to come back and bite me. Tomorrow I was going to set off on my first ever cycle adventure and begin a month of actual exercise, something I hadn't done for quite a while.

In hindsight, Sambuca is probably the exact thing you shouldn't do but we all make mistakes. Don't judge me. We took up the entire corner of a pub, an Irish pub that used to be a church. How ironic. Hundreds of people going to church every day to get drunk. What's happened to us? Only the Irish could get away with that. Although no true Irishman would be caught dead in this commercial cliché of Ireland all geared to the average English punter who has some distant cousin in Ireland. Plastic Paddy's is what they call them. I can talk though. I have an Irish passport but have only ever been there 3 times.

We were situated right above the Altar on the upper deck overlooking the rest of the pub below, which still has

7

the reminiscence of smoke stained walls from before the smoking ban came in. After the cheering ended, there seemed to be a pause in time as the whole pub stopped what they were doing to look over at us and then as if a glitch in the matrix, the play button on society was pressed and everything carried on as normal.

I was really impressed that so many of my friends had made the effort to come to my leaving drinks on a random Thursday. Some came from as far as Tunbridge Wells, a good 2 hours away just to say hi. (And feed me Sambuca.) It was all a bit overwhelming.

We were eventually kicked out at closing time and in a haze caused by the efforts of my friends trying (and succeeding) to get as much booze down me as possible, I staggered home. It was a little way down the hill to my flat. I don't remember any of it.

I later found out I phoned about 5 people, one being my friend in America. Why I still do the drunken phone calls around the world, I don't know? The last thing I can remember was looking at my cheap, over bright alarm clock. It lights up my entire room. What a design flaw. It read 2 am and I had to be up at 7 am. Oh dear!

Who am I? My name is Sean but my friends call me Conners and apart from wanting an adventure, I also need to get out of the big smog. I feel the concrete jungle is suffocating me. With that I have decided to take a whole month off to cycle the length of Britain for charity. My 1300(ish) mile trip will start from Land's End and head all the way up to Scotland. Whenever I tell people this, their

first response is:
"But that's all up-hill mate."
I am getting this response so often I am starting to think that maybe they could be right. I was never very good at geography. I really hope it's not all uphill. I have not planned anything and only bought a bike a few months ago for the trip.

I am heading off with no idea of where I am going to stay or any idea of a route. Most people who do this ride stay in B&Bs, but I have decided to camp the whole way. Just myself (obviously), a tent (and other camping gear), some maps, and a Lonely Planet guide book.

I have decided to do the ride in April, the end of winter, before the rush of tourists hit the road. That's about the only planning I've done - cycle when it's not going to be busy. Great!

Anyway. Too much planning makes you miss opportunities. I'm completely making that up to feel better really because I literally know nothing about cycling or Britain. Oh well. Onwards and upwards – hopefully, not literally!

In my garden in London ready to go

Little Flying Cow

London to Penzance

My alarm kicks my arse out of bed at 7 am.
"Oh my head." I blurt out, only to hear a rough giggle from the lounge. My flatmate had made secret bets with himself whether or not I would make it up in time to get my train.
"Damn it! Were you responsible for my head-ache?"
The memories of last night still a dream-like haze.
"No man, it was all Matt's fault."
"Remind me to kick his arse," I grunt. My voice still trying to wake up. I sound like Johnny Cash. Nice.

I had put everything for my trip on the sofa the day before where it still lay all muddled up. I had been so busy trying to wrap up last minute shoots that I didn't have much time to pack. (When I say shoots, I mean photo shoots and not some secret mission for MI5. I'm a photographer.) I looked at each individual item spread over my sofa to make sure it deserved a righteous place on my bicycle. I need to keep the weight as low as possible.

The Kit List

1x Dawes Horizon touring bicycle. 21 speed.
1x sleeping bag with a -15 degree comfort rating.
1x one-man tent
1x gas stove

2x cooking pans
1x plastic cup
2x underwear
2x socks(pairs, not just 5 socks)
2x t-shirts
1x jeans for evenings in the pub
1x warm coat for getting to the pub
1x rucksack for clothes. Also doubles as a pillow.
1x British Lonely Planet guide book
1x camping guide
50 pages of relevant maps for the trip.
1x pair of trainers
5x panniers. 2 front, 2 back and 1 on the handlebars.
1x spare tube
2x spare chain links
1x tyre pump
1x Leatherman Multi-tool
1x cycle tool kit
2x locks - A u-lock and a stretchy one.
2x water bottles
1x towel
1x toothbrush
1x toothpaste
1x deodorant (I figured shampoo and soap were a luxury I didn't have space for)
1x toilet paper, which I never used but kept religiously for the 'just in case' moment. I was not prepared to use dried grass again – long story.
1x 12 mega pixel digital SLR camera
1x point and shoot digital
1x MP3 player

1x mascot. The Little Flying Cow, which I have tied to the top of my handlebars. He is not so much flying as just splayed out in a superman pose with both front arms (or legs?) facing forward and back legs out backwards. He has a light hazel skin with big black eyes and small white horns just coming through some fluff on his head. So small that he would definitely lose the fight to become big daddy in the herd, therefore never acquiring the rights to the beautiful lady cows in his paddock. He looked so vulnerable sitting at the back of a pile of toys in a charity shop located right next door to the Irish church pub, I just had to take him.

As midday hangovers are the new craze I was slowly starting to feel worse by the minute. This state of dreamlike numbness would increase rapidly until the stroke of midday when it would seem to disappear altogether. I would then spend the next 2 hours trying to work out what was dream and what was reality, while getting small glimpses of embarrassing events from the previous night. I still have a very long train journey to deal with. Let's just concentrate on getting to the train first, shall we?

I was too tired to pack properly so just shoved everything into my panniers in no particular order. Over the next 25 days, I had an exact place for everything and my packing/unpacking strategy would save me an hour each day. Small consistencies become very important when you spend the best part of a month alone.

I battled down the stairs with Valerie. That's what I called my bike. I originally went with Bob the Bike but was worried about the reaction I would get from small town folk if my opening line was:

"Hi, nice to meet you. Sorry I am walking like this, but I have been riding Bob all day."

That is why I went for Valerie. She was one of my very first school crushes and I recently met up with her for the first time in over 10 years. She was more stunning than ever. I think my trip will be made easier if I think of her every time I have to get up and cycle in the rain. There will be no perverted jokes about 'Riding Valerie' either, thank you very much.

My train from Paddington leaves at 10 am. It's at least 8 miles down into town with only a small uphill to start but then a very easy ride past Hampstead Heath. I give myself 90 minutes just in case I feel ill on the way and have to rush into a bush.

As I am heading out of Muswell Hill, I get a few hoots from people driving past. I don't want to let go of the handlebars just yet, so instead of a wave I just give the drivers a polite head bow in appreciation. They must have seen the articles in one or another local paper, or they saw me falling over in the pub last night. Please be the paper. Please.

I am still a bit shaky on the bike due to how heavy she is. Yes, it's definitely the weight. Nothing to do with my hangover, I convince myself.

Cycling between Highgate Woods and Queens Woods and then on to Hampstead Heath is a very nice way to start my trip. It starts to rain. The coolness of the water running down my face is very refreshing though. It still hadn't quite sunk in that I am going to be on my bike for a whole month. Every single day. All day. Scary and exciting – like tightrope walking without the risk of dying part.

I wasn't ill and got to Paddington with an hour to spare. The typical hustle and bustle of a busy train station was in full swing, with the majority of people not even seeing me as I try and navigate my bike through the hordes of temporary blind people. This, despite the fact I have printed on my fluorescent cycling vest the words 'I'm cycling the length of Britain for Charity.' And then the words 'Talk to me', in a funky little speech bubble. Bloody busy city. I can't wait to get away.

The smell of coffee from the small coffee van is too much to ignore, so I head over and get the usual medium latte and then sit down on one of only 5 free seats. The cold metal chair sends shock waves up to my fragile head.

I love people watching. There are some great characters wandering around. Firstly there is the classic city broker kid, mid 20's and already on £50,000 a year. Almost always wearing a pink tie and walking with a slight cocky attitude, they have the worst temporary blindness of all. I have called them simply; Pink Ties.

A favourite to watch are the tourists who have never been to a big city before and made the grave mistake of booking a rush hour train from the airport. They are always looking up at least 20 degrees higher than your average Pink Tie while seemingly wandering in circles around the station trying in vain to find out which exit to take. Most of them seem to spend 20 minutes getting lost, rather than ask someone for fear of 'looking like a tourist'. How ironic.

It's amazing how pigeons manage to make it into a predominantly enclosed station. They have become the most streetwise of all the pigeons. A category parallel in the human world to the street kids of Rio. The pigeons strut their stuff and seemingly manage to dodge every person walking at them and only make the effort to fly at the very last minute when there is nowhere to go. This is usually when some Pink Tie has a go at kicking one of the little buggers. They never get them and give a disgruntled short sigh as they carry on striding through the crowds.

A lot can be learned about a city if you spend an hour in a train station. It's kind of like reading the back of a book: getting a glimpse of what to expect once you get in. It's great! In my hour in Paddington, I came up with the already known conclusion that central London is Stress City.

Finally my platform is up on the board and I make my down to the very far end to where the cycle carriage is. It takes me a good 15 minutes to secure Valerie (which is not allowed) to the inside of the carriage so that she doesn't fall over. My seat number is miles down the other end of the train so I chance it and find an unreserved seat near my bike.

The carriage is fairly empty and I have a free seat next to me. I am pretty tired but my excitement is keeping me wide awake. That and the fact that my medium latte has started to kick in. 10.05 am and the train releases its brakes with a puff of pressure. This makes my heart race as I know that the train is about to set off and my trip is about to begin. The platform starts to float past the window next to me as we head out of the station gaining speed as we go west.

The tack-itty-tack of the wheels are increasing in frequency until matching the rhythm of my worryingly fast hungover heartbeat. This is it. My short 3 months of training, (well when I say training I mean I started cycling to work and back which was 10 miles,) has rushed by and the beginning of what would be one of the most exciting months of my life so far has begun.

The guy next to me has the longest dreads in the world for a white man. Seriously! They go all the way to his knees with the bottom part showing his original hair colour and getting greyer all the way up to his head where he is now predominantly all grey.

He is covered in tattoos which were clearly done 100 years ago by some back alley artist and starting to fade. His girlfriend also has a few tattoos but they were done more recently and looked a hell of a lot better. They must be going somewhere exciting together for he is behaving in a very excitable hyperactive manner. The way we all do if we know we are about to go somewhere fun.

He tries to kiss his girlfriend who is giving him the 'You need to work harder for my affection' treatment. (Us boys love that by the way girls!) She turns away, yet he persists. He tries so hard that he spills his Strongbow cider all over himself. I couldn't contain my laughter and resorted to watching the proceedings from the reflection in my window so as to hide my smile. The laughter is making my head throb but it is so worth it. Also Strongbow? It's 10 am!

Tack-itty-tack, tack-itty-tack, as the buildings get smaller and further apart until all I can see is the wide-open countryside. I start to get comfortable and munch on an overpriced BLT sandwich I bought in the station. As I take the biggest bite, I hear a little voice from an old lady.

"Morning, is this seat taken?"

Oh no. It can't be. Just when I thought I was going to get away with putting my feet up.

"Sorry?" I asked with my mouth full, hoping she might see another seat that takes her fancy.

"This seat. Is it free, dear?" She asked again.

"Of course. Let me just move my bag."

I moved it under the seat in front of me. Don't make eye contact, I think to myself. That's the key. Just keep looking out the window and you'll be fine. She sat down and her mothball smelling clothes damn near knocked me out. I leant forward to get a tissue and realised my mistake simultaneously as I heard.

"Wow, that's so wonderful. You are a good person."

The old lady was holding her glasses up to her eyes, trying to read everything on the back of my cycle vest, her mouth open and frowning. Like that makes you read better, I thought irritably.

"Thank you," I smiled.

"What charity are you doing it for?" She asked inquisitively.

"The Campaign to Protect Rural England."

"Mmmmmm, I support the Cancer fund." She said as if her charity was a more important one. "My husband had cancer you see, and it cost a lot of money to help him get better."

"How is he now?" I asked.

"Oh no dear, he is dead." She said as if a matter of fact.

I almost choked on another bite of my BLT sandwich.

"I am so sorry."

"Ha-ha. He didn't die from the cancer. Just good old

fashioned old age got the better of him. If there is a charity to cure old age, I would support that one too."

She had clearly come to terms with his death and didn't show any signs of awkwardness at all.

"Me too," is all I could think of saying, hoping by keeping my answer brief would end the conversation, which ironically made me more uncomfortable than her.

"That's so wonderful what you are doing. Really, is it. Where are you going to?"

"My train is heading to Penzance."

"Oh lovely. The scenery is splendid." Her voice getting excitable as if she had so much to tell me.

"I think I may miss most of it, as I am really tired because of my leaving party last night. I only went to bed at 2 am."

I was hoping she might get the hint and allow me to sleep. She didn't! In fact I don't think she even heard me.

"I remember taking the train to Penzance with my husband. We had a jolly good time bird watching and walking along the beach. The sunsets in Cornwall are splendid. Splendid they are."

She talked without looking at me and clutching her reading glasses in both her hands, which were placed neatly on her lap.

"I am really looking forward to it. I have never been before," I said trying to hide my headache.

There was a short silence while she still thought about old times when she was happiest. I took the opportunity as I knew I might not get another one.

"I am really sorry, but I really need to get some sleep. I am rather tired. It was great chatting with you," I said slowly, trying to be as eloquent as possible.

Her disappointment was clear and I felt incredibly guilty.

"Oh, OK dear. You get your sleep in. You are going to need your strength for sure."

I smiled and put my headphones on and lay flat on the cold fold-down table. It smelled of beer. I bet someone else had been trying to kiss their girlfriend and spilled their beer too. The thought made me smile as I drifted off.

When I awoke, I saw the little old lady had moved seats and was now interrogating some other chap. I felt really bad that I had dismissed her. That is such a Londoner thing to do. She had now moved down the carriage and I didn't even get her name.

Then I realised with a sudden shock about all the Guinness I had last night and we know what that does to your bowels. I hope I didn't stink her out in my sleep. Please God no! I subconsciously prayed.

I was too embarrassed to make eye contact with her, so just watched the scenery go by. I figured we were in Devon by now. The old lady was right. The scenery was splendid.

The train pulled into Penzance at around 3.30 pm. It had rained earlier but it seemed to have cleared up a bit. I have decided to cycle to Land's End this afternoon to feel as if I have at least achieved something today.

I untie Valerie who hasn't moved an inch. Not sure that would have been the case if I had not tied her up. I leave the station and it starts to rain slightly which I hardly notice as I am still concentrating on staying on the road. Valerie is very slow with all the weight she is carrying, -

40kgs including the bike I think.

The road climbs through the town where many people are staring at me. I have attached a flagpole to the back of Valerie where I have attached 3 Tibetan prayer flags. A red, green and yellow one. The flags and the fact that I probably have the most crap on a bicycle anyone has ever seen make people very inquisitive but very rarely satisfy their questioning minds and approach me. Humans can be funny sometimes.

I headed out of town and soon find myself struggling against a huge headwind. I am tired and haven't eaten much today which makes things worse. It's only 9 miles to Land's End but it takes me nearly 2 hours. Each pedal motion is taking a lot of energy and I have to rest every 30 metres or so on the up hills. I was blown completely off the road at some points. I start singing the first song that comes into my mind but change the words accordingly.

"Well I will cycle 1000 miles, and I will cycle 1000 more. Just to be the man that cycled 1000 miles . . . . ."

I suddenly stop singing as I nearly re-run over some road kill. As if the little badger hasn't had enough bad luck, I damn nearly go and put a thin line across his stomach just to top it off. The little swerve and dodge has landed me half way into the low-lying hedge, which is not helping in any way to shield the wind.

"This is going to be tough Little Flying Cow." I say out loud and then realise I am talking to a toy. Am I going mad already?

I reach Land's End only to find that it's the tackiest place I have ever seen. It's also off-season so there is no one around. All it needed was a few tumbleweeds to complete its eeriness.

The wind is so strong I can taste the salt from the sea blowing into my face. Even the photography company that takes your photo hadn't even bothered to come to work today. It is truly a grim start to the trip. At least I have a bit of a tailwind heading back to Penzance.

I turn around straight after taking a few photos just to prove I was there and headed back to one of the campsites a few miles away. I hadn't even thought what I was going to do for dinner so stop at an Off-Licence and get some canned vegetable soup and some bulk standard rice. I am going to attempt cooking. This should be fun.

I find a campsite about 4 miles down the road. It's surprisingly cheap at £4.50 per night. What a bargain. I was soon to realise that the price really reflected the facilities. No hot water and pretty appalling ablutions. Hey! I am not here to live it up in luxury. I am really looking forward to camping though. It's been way too long since I last slept in a tent.

My tent is a small lightweight one-man tent, bright green in colour. There are two openings, one in the front where there is a little porch area and another along the side for easy access. It only takes two poles to erect (tent poles and not people from Eastern Europe) and is up in less than 5 minutes, with practice. I however have had no practice and spend half an hour in the bleeding wind trying to figure out which pole goes where. As a rookie I let it go for a second to fetch the pegs. When I turn around, it's half way across the field.

"Crap!"

I run after it and it seems to be playing games with me. As I get near to pick it up, it decides to do a runner again.

"Stop messing with me, I don't have the energy." I curse.

This happened 2 or 3 times before the hedge on the far side of the field stops it from going any further. Now the battle to drag it all the way back to the other side of the field a good 50 metres away. I almost take off Mary Poppins style. I eventually get it all sorted and settle in for my first night in. I snuggle into the tent and realise just how small it is. I can't even sit up without banging my head on one of the poles. I loved it though. It was cosy.

The sounds remind me of my African days. The pitter-patter of the rain and wind blowing the nylon tent sheets together soon sends me into a deep sleep.

Day one is over. 24 to go.

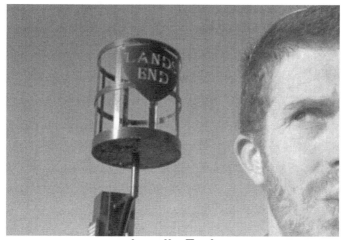

Land's End

First night camping

Penzance to Tencreek

6 am - I didn't sleep at all well, but seem refreshed nonetheless. I am awoken by a herd of cows having a deep conversation with each other about this green tent they see next to their field. There are 5 of them, all standing in a row along the fence looking at me. One of them looks a lot like Little Flying Cow but with bigger horns.

The wind has died down but it is bloody cold. My body starts to shiver uncontrollably as I change into my warm cycling clothes. My teeth are chattering and if I close my eyes, I imagine a war zone with machine-guns firing at will.

My stomach feels empty and I can't wait for a fry-up in Penzance. Packing up seems a breeze without um . . . a *breeze* in the air and I am on my bike in no time.

As I leave the field I give my friendly alarm clock cows a few hoots with my old school bike horn. The horn was a present from a friend and whenever I squeeze it, it makes me chuckle. Small things amuse small minds.

The trip back to Penzance seems a lot faster than last night. I arrive even before the main cafés are open so head towards the harbour to find some food.

My stomach is starting to eat itself. There must be some early bird fishermen needing breakfast too. My gut feeling was right. It seems I have a unique skill to find food: a skill that has saved me from starvation a good few times since.

I found a small porter cabin, which had one old man behind the counter. He didn't speak much and just wrote my self-designed order on his little bit of paper: 3 eggs, 2 bacons and 1 sausage. This became known simply as the 3-2-1 breakfast. I got my wallet out to pay and he waved his hand at me as if to say, "Go and sit."

What did he mean? Do I pay later, or is it possible that he is not charging me for my meal. There is no way I would have the luck to get my very first meal for free. Confused, I went and sat down in the corner. I always sit in corners of pubs, restaurants or cafés. I don't know why, but I just like to observe as much as I can without anyone observing me without me knowing. I like to remain understated as much as possible. I then laughed at my own theory for I was sitting in a café with a bright fluorescent jacket on. I couldn't have stood out more if I tried.

I ate as if I hadn't seen food in years and it was only after I finished that I noticed a good few people staring at me.

"Hey! Are you finished or just starting?" said one of the fishermen sitting in the corner by himself. He was clearly drained from a morning's fishing and still in denial from the days when the fishing market was booming.

"I have just started." I said, while wiping ketchup from the corner of my mouth. My body language becoming more like that of someone attending an interview for a job they didn't really know much about.

"So, a long way to go then."

"Oh! Yes. I am zigzagging up over the next month."

"So you are not going straight up?" Someone else asked from a nearby table that was also interested in my trip.

"Nope." I said now relaxing a bit, comfortable that I have won my audience over. Everyone in the café was now listening intensely. I thought this would be a good time to mention the charity to them as someone was bound to ask.

"I am cycling for the Campaign to Protect Rural England."

"So what about Scotland?" said another old lady in the corner.

I looked over to her, my body re-posing into interview mode. I was relieved to see her smiling jokingly.

"Just kidding, my boy, that's wonderful, just wonderful."

She sounded just like the old lady on the train. Maybe they were sisters. We all chatted for the next few minutes while I finished my coffee and the whole atmosphere was brilliant. Even people entering the café soon had smiles on their faces. It's amazing how positive energy can transcend through a crowd.

After I finished my coffee, I headed up to pay and the old man looked confused.

"Don't worry," he said, while signalling the same hand movement from before.

"Wow! Thank you so much. That's very kind of you."

I turned around to a sea of eyes all staring at me, with smiles on their faces.

"Cheers everyone. Wish me luck."

"Good luck!" They all seemed to say in unison.

This was a good start to my trip.

I headed out of Penzance and onto a 'B' road heading along the coast. My good start was short-lived as a huge headwind hit me smack in the face. There is no way wind can be this strong. After 20 minutes and 2 road kill rabbits later, I had to stop on the side of the road for a rest.

It had started to rain and I couldn't feel my feet. Imagine a hamster on a running wheel. Now put the wheel in a shower and turn it on full blast. Then get an industrial fan and put it 20 cm from the hamster. Then to top it off, put the wheel in a bowl of syrup. Not the thin Maple stuff, but rather the thick Lyle's Golden which you need a knife to get at.

Now you get an idea of how difficult it is to cycle along the coast away from Penzance. My legs were really burning. At times, I had to lean 45 degrees to compensate for the side winds that must have been over 500mph, surely?

I am starting to think that I may not enjoy this trip. I could be in Hawaii right now. Sitting on a beach drinking a dry martini with a few slices of lemon, which I wouldn't have to ask for because the bar lady would know my order as soon as she saw me approaching the thatched beachside shack creatively named 'Beachside Bar'.

"No! This is all part of the adventure." I said to myself.

Little Flying Cow was drenched and the little tufts of hair on his head were flat ,almost blinding him. I moved them away so he could see where we were going. I didn't want him to be left out. The cycling improved a bit and the dual carriageway helped a bit in getting the miles in.

By lunchtime I arrive in a lovely town called Truro, a beautiful market town. The old architecture and narrow pavements bring a calming effect to my fairly windswept morning. I love old English towns. There is a massive downhill into the centre and I only hope I don't have to go back up it to get out. My legs are truly tired from the hamster-syrup cycling. I stop to find a place in the Lonely Planet. I can't find anything, so wander through the market for inspiration.

There are many people interested in my trip and I have to repeat my story about 7 times about how far I have come, where I am heading, what charity, etc. Country folk are so much friendlier. It's taking a bit of getting used to the whole idea of random people coming up to me. I even get a free cup of soup. Local butternut broth. Mmmmmm! It filled a small hole but I currently need to eat the equivalent of 6 billion burgers a day just to recoup the calories I am burning, so I headed off for a big lasagne in a local Italian restaurant. Bring on carbohydrates.

After lunch and a few more episodes of story telling and £4.23 in random donations, I left Truro heading roughly in the direction of Scotland. Hopefully. The Cornish countryside is incredible but very, very hilly.

Maybe everyone was right. It must be all uphill. My lack of preparation is evident, and my lack of training makes for slow going. At least the small green lanes, which are so unused they practically have a forest running down the centre, are very scenic and keep my mind from thinking about my burning legs.

Hill, after hill, after hill, takes its toll on my knees and by 4 pm it's time to find a campsite. Luckily, and not planned at all, my map shows where all the campsites are located. Result. Not actually sure what I would have done otherwise. Didn't think that part through.

The closest one is in Tencreek and guess what, it has,

wait for it, a hot shower. I was camping in the middle of a farm with loads of animals. I hope the bloody chickens don't wake me up at 4 am. I would have to cook one if that happens.

I managed to do a better job at setting up camp. The wind was still howling so I found a space between two caravans. It kind of worked.

Dinner was a soggy pizza in the campsite restaurant. I also tried a local cider. The local barmaid was something out of a Roald Dahl book. She was quite overweight, and very grumpy. Her only attempt to seduce a tip out of anyone was to wear a pretty low cut top to reveal her quadruple D assets while bending over to serve me my cider. I accepted gladly while keeping eye contact and took a huge gulp. It's safe to say I was a bit disappointed when it tasted like someone left apple juice in a jar for 4 months and then drained it through a sumo wrestler's crack. It also came in a 750cl bottle so I had 45 minutes of hell pretending it was indeed the 'best in the world' so as not to upset grumpy top-heavy barmaid. After my last sip, she started to open another one.

"Another one sir?"

"No! Um, I mean no, thank you. I must be off to bed for an early start." I said.

"Oh OK. No bother."

Her disappointment was clear. Partly as I was the only one in the restaurant and she wanted to double her takings for the evening, and partly that I had rejected an offer for the best cider in the world. Pheewwee! Close one.

Lying in bed, my mind is still crazy-hyperactive and it's clear I still haven't de-stressed from London. Eventually tiredness soon overcomes and I fall asleep.

Camping Supplies

Another quaint British village

Tencreek to Dartmoor

It's sunny!!!! Yay! I slept really well but am starting to think I bought a tent that is a little too small. For sleeping it's OK but you can't do anything else in it - like change clothes if it's raining outside.

There is ice on my tent and even though my hands are freezing, I still feel in high spirits for the day ahead. I saw The Eden Project on the map so I am going to head there this morning. It only opens at 10 am, so I have some time to kill.

I had some coffee and headed out into the morning mist. The valleys to each side of me were scattered with strangely clean sheep in bright green fields. Steam coming out with their every breath.

"What should we do now Little Flying Cow?" I asked out loud, and then felt like an idiot for doing so.

Strangely as soon I asked I thought that taking a detour through the country lanes would be nice. Weird? Had Little Flying Cow talked to me or was it coincidence I had thought of something the second I asked him. It's as if he is my alter ego and is trying to make this trip as adventurous as possible.

The green lanes to The Eden Project were smooth and quiet, but very steep. Most of them consisted of at least 3 rest stops on the way up. I was almost there with still an hour to spare so decided to do some off-roading.

I saw an old medieval castle on a hill (It was actually just an old mill but in my mind it was a castle) and decided I needed to get there. Once a challenge presented itself, there was no turning back. I headed up a green lane lined with 6-foot high bramble.

The road seemed to go on forever and I couldn't find a way into the field to get to the mill, I mean castle. The further I went without finding an entrance, the more I needed to get there. I was on a new mini adventure within my big adventure. I could hardly stand the excitement.

Eventually I found a small wooden gate and went through. I was now in the field and all that lay between me and my castle was 200m of thick, wet mud.

"Come on Little Flying Cow, we can do this."

Valerie's wheels cut through the mud like a hot knife through butter and she started to wheel spin.

"The hamster in the wheel has returned." I thought.

"But I shall go on!" I said out loud in a Mel Gibson style from Braveheart.

Then laughed at myself, and thought how ridiculous I must have looked if someone was watching me. I looked around and could only see a few sheep glancing my way. I nodded my head as if to say hi and carried on the struggle. I could feel the mud clogging up my chain and going all up my back. I loved it.

I reached the old mill and let Valerie rest for a bit. I suddenly realised how quiet it was. So still, and perfect! A few starlings were sitting on the top of the only chimney left to get the first of the morning rays. How calm and peaceful - and exactly what I needed. I could feel the stress leaving my body as the sun rose above the mist.

I arrived at the Eden Project half an hour early so stopped at the top of the hill overlooking the place. It looked incredible. The bio-dome containing the rain forest was huge and I can't contain my excitement. The smell of flowers drifting up the hill along with the rising mist sends me into a parallel world of make believe. The gigantic bee on the side of the hill seems to start to hum. Little Flying Cow is mooing away. This is definitely the furthest away from Stress City so far and I love it. As my mind is beginning to wander I hear a rough voice saying:

"Bloody monstrosity, isn't it?"

I turned to see a middle aged lady with purple hair walking her bull terrier.

"Morning," I sang, still high from the mornings activities.

"It's never been the same since those things, those huge ugly things came here," she says, pointed to the two bio-domes while screwing up her face like a 5-year old would at the sight of broccoli.

"Oh! Really?"

"Yes, I used to be able to walk my dog along the green lanes but now there are hundreds of busses and cars all polluting the air with car fumes and noise and . . and . . .and car fumes!"

I never thought of this, but I guess she has a point. She carried on.

"It's just a big money making scheme."

"But what about the charity they raise funds for?" I interrupted

"It all goes into their back pockets to fund holidays to the Caribbean."

"Oh really?" I couldn't be bothered for an argument so

decided to go with it. I was in too good a mood and could feel her negativity draining me already. "Maybe you should recommend they use electric busses like they use at the Taj Mahal. This would cut the pollution wouldn't it?"

"That wouldn't do anything. There would still be cars."

I could see she was getting agitated with the whole scenario. I couldn't understand why she just doesn't move. Surely moving half a mile over the hill would solve her problems. Humans love to complain but never actually take actions to solve their problems.

"What time is it?" I asked changing the subject.

"10.05am."

"Great! Well, I gotta run. It was great meeting you."

I made a swift exit and freewheeled down the hill to the entrance. Although still in a fairly good mood, the purple haired lady had made me think that maybe it wasn't all it was made out to be.

My questioning mind was soon put to rest when I entered the rain forest bio-dome. The smells and sounds took me right back to Africa. Wandering through the different paths, recognising sounds and plants, and breathing in the heavy saturated air reminded me of my childhood. It was very humid and small balls of moisture started condensing on my forehead. I was in my own little world again. The purple haired lady was a far distant illusion who made no sense. I loved it.

I started to think of my life in Africa and how I had managed to find my way to one of the biggest cities in the world. Was I better off back in Africa? I was born in Zimbabwe and my Dad was a game ranger. A real game ranger. He kicks the arse out of Crocodile Dundee. With

Dad being a game ranger, I spent all my childhood in the bush with no TV, 2 hours of electricity and only a pet warthog, 2 dogs and some ducks for company. Life seemed so simple out there.

Waking up to elephants in your garden and sunsets that looked like a painting were part of everyday life. Oh, how I miss it more and more as I get older. Africa wasn't without its problems though. We loved dogs and kept at least 2 at a time as inevitably one a year would get eaten or poisoned. When I was about 18 months old, our first dog, in fact it was most of our pets, died on one weekend. The dog, Shamwari, was eaten by a crocodile while trying to swim to our boat. She just disappeared in a small splash. There wasn't even a fight. I don't remember anything at all but Mum always has a few tears telling the story. She loved Shamwari.

After the boat incident, Mum, Dad and I drove the bumpy dirt road home to find a python in the duck cage. The bloody thing had eaten all the ducks and ducklings. You could still see the bumps in the python's stomach. Seriously! Africa was harsh but I loved it and sometimes wish I hadn't left. Oh, and a leopard ate the cat too. At least that's what we think. She just disappeared, never to be seen again.

I didn't want to leave The Eden Project either but knew I had far to go. I left feeling happy and although I understood purple haired lady's ideas, I came to the conclusion that the educational benefit from such a place far outshone the negatives.

I need to get to Dartmoor tonight. It's not too far and hopefully there aren't too many hills.

20 minutes later . . .

There *are* too many hills, and not just your average slope either, bloody great mountains. It must be all uphill. Why didn't I look into this? I should have started in Scotland instead. All I used were two gears. Bradley Wiggins gear for the downhills and Granny gear for the inevitable uphills. My legs felt like jelly and I was starting to lose concentration.

"It's not looking good mate."

I am talking to a toy? He seems to answer my questions for me. It's also better than talking to myself . . . or is it?

"Just think of joke and that would cheer you up."

Just then I cycled through the biggest cowpat I have ever seen.

"Ah crap, that's so your fault. Look what your kind has done."

It really stank which nearly made me crash. A real fresh one!

"Keep awake, Conners. Seriously!"

I reached Tavistock at around 6 pm. I can't tell you much about the town because all I could focus on was finding food, fatty, salty, unhealthy food. Bring it on!

It wasn't long before I found a pub, which served the biggest cheeseburger I have ever seen. I'm convinced they shipped it in from America. Cows don't grow that big here in the UK. My burger experience was helped by the fact the waitress looked like she came straight out of modelling school.

I sat there, pretty content with life.

It was an hour before I realised I should probably find a place to camp tonight. I looked on the map and see that

Dartmoor was just over the hill. It would be brilliant to stay there the night. I am not sure if it's legal but I don't care.

I head up into Dartmoor but am quickly disappointed to find fences lining the roads with only a few stiles for people to climb over to get onto the moor. Surely it's not all like this. My legs are killing me and I am going about 5 miles an hour. It's also getting dark and cold. Just as I am about to give up and head back to a campsite, I see an opening ahead.

"Yeah baby!" I shout and a sudden urge of energy gets me out of the green lanes and onto the open plains of Dartmoor.

The sun drops below the darkening clouds, which sends glowing rays and dramatic shadows across the landscape. I stop for a second to take it all in. There is a small stream next to me, which would be a great place to camp. I head off the road and follow the river about 500 metres down to where I find a clump of trees. It is perfect. The sound of water, the green grass and looming clouds all add to the sense of adventure.

I set up camp pretty quickly and sit back to appreciate my home for the night. I found a patch of wet leaves to use as a mattress under my tent (forgot to buy a camping matt) and the branches above provided suitable support for my ropes. Swallows overhead signify that it's probably going to rain so I decide to go for a quick stroll along the river before dark. There is no one around. I love it.

The crystal clear stream dances through the grassy wetland carefully dodging its way through moss covered rocks. I wash my face in the cold water and all thoughts about my jelly legs have gone. The first drops of rain hit my head as I wander back to the tent. I am probably the most tired I have been since the trip began and as the rain on my tent gets louder I fall into a deep dark sleep.

"Get up! Hurry! Hurry!"

I rush out of my tent to find myself in a pool of water. Valerie has been swept away and I am on a small island surrounded by a raging torrent. I try and run but the tent ropes I tied to the tree have entangled me. I am stuck with the water raging higher and higher. The water is reaching my neck and . . .

The Eden Project

Camping wild on Dartmoor

Dartmoor to Exeter

I wake up with a sudden jolt and in sitting up, hit my head on the top pole of the tent and fall straight back down again. OK, this tent is too small. A dream, it was only a dream. I look outside to make sure. Phew! Only a dream! Must have been the 7kgs of cheese I had on that burger last night. Cheese dreams are always crazy.

It's 7 am and bloody raining again. No one told me it rains in England. Honestly! I did however have the best sleep so far. That wet leaf mattress seriously worked. Mental note. Need to get a mattress.

I pack up camp and head into the middle of Dartmoor. I am hoping to find some early breakfast in Princetown but the going is very slow. Valerie is heavy and I need food. My legs are burning and I have to stop twice on all the hills as I make my way up into the moor. That's one less than yesterday though. Whoop! I'm getting fitter already.

I knew I should have done some training for this. It takes me 2 hours to do 6 miles, but I eventually reached Princetown. There is a massive prison here, which hasn't had an escapee in years. They usually get caught half way into the moor. I also read that the prisoners that died were buried in the moor. That's quite spooky. Maybe they were buried near where I camped and that's why I had a crazy dream?

I found a small café and have another 3-2-1 breakfast

and a cup of tea. I don't know why I ordered tea. I prefer coffee, but it just seemed the thing to do when in a quaint English café. After a good feed, I feel like a new man and decide I really need to focus on eating properly. It makes such a difference.

Cycling through Dartmoor was beautiful. The purple heather clad moors, rolling hills and ancient towns dating back to the 10th century take me back to the days when people first discovered this land.

It was probably in the prehistoric era when dinosaurs roamed free. (Was there ever a charge for roaming?) How cool would it be to see a Tyrannosaurus Rex chasing some cows through the moor? They wouldn't have a chance. (Sorry Little Flying Cow. God knows how you lot survived!) There are also hundreds of sheep and it gives me great pleasure in scaring them with my horn, which sends them running down the slippery slope. I'm going to hell!

I forgot to fill my water bottles in Princetown, so decide to take a break and fill them up in the river. The cool stream send shivers down my neck as I grab handfuls of the crystal clear water. It tastes almost sweet. I don't think I will be able to drink London water again after this.

I don't want to leave Dartmoor. I want to find a small clump of trees and build a shack and stay there forever, living off the land.

Cycling through the rest of Dartmoor is slow. It's starting to rain again which I'm getting a little bored with already. I arrive in Moretonhampstead, another beautiful quaint English town, and follow the signs for Exeter, which is 12 miles away. Not bad. I should be there by mid afternoon.

After half an hour of cycling I hit a huge Motorway. What? That's not on the map. Crap! I stopped and asked directions, only to find out I am now 15 miles from Exeter and I have just done 6 miles.

"Idiot." I curse

"Yes you are." Little Flying Cow was in agreement.

"Shut up you or I will leave you in that ditch," I pointed to a ditch full of bramble.

Little Flying Cow seemed to be laughing at me from my handlebars and that annoyed me. I was going to have to cycle on the dreaded A30 to Exeter. A huge dual carriageway 'A' road with loads of trucks and dirty car fumes.

There's no point in delaying the inevitable, so I tighten up my cycle jacket and get on with it. The going is fast paced but I can hardly think because of all the trucks speeding past me. A few give me a hoot or two which helps, but the rest just fly past almost taking me with them in their slip-stream.

I reached Exeter in good time and almost got run over only once. I thought that to be quite good for busy town traffic. I was hoping to bypass the city, all cities for that matter, but need food and it's time to find a place to sleep.

As there are no campsites available, I have decided to spend the night in a hostel. I have been put in a dorm of 12 people. It feels really cramped and claustrophobic. There are some real characters here too.

At the dining table there are all the traveller egos telling their best travel tales trying to one-up each other. It's quite amusing as I have heard all these stories a million times over. Really, you would think bringing out the 'Yeah, so I lived in Kathmandu for a month' story is old hat by now. Who hasn't done that? Actually, I haven't. But that's not the point. Loads of people have. Choose a better story.

Then there is the token Oriental who can't speak a word of English and just sits in the corner watching TV which he blatantly can't understand yet seems to be glued to. In the lounge are the lads (who must be builders from Eastern Europe) who live in the hostel permanently and look upon us folk as flies encroaching on their cake. Why on earth would you live here? It's not even cheap.

Lastly there are the group of 'mature' travellers who, for whatever reason, decide to start travelling in their late 50's. They are the most interesting, and travel to places they want to and not to the places the 'Ego Travellers' go, just to get the stamp in the passport. My favourite was Sophie from Australia or dare I say New Zealand. Seriously? Can anyone actually tell the difference? Judging by her dress style and developing wrinkles, she must be in her early 50's.

"Alright kiddo, so what's your story then?" She seemed genuinely interested in me.

"I am cycling the length of Britain for charity."

"Fair dinkum, that's bonza."

She said bonza, I almost fell off my chair. I thought that was an Australian cliché. Kind of like 'throw another shrimp on the barbie' which no self-righteous Australian would ever say according to my other flatmate.

"I am enjoying it, it's good fun so far. No major accidents."

"Good on ya. Where are ya heading? Are ya almost finished or just gettin' started?"

"Just started and a long way to go."

"Ha-ha," she laughed and took off her green jumper to get comfortable. I could tell she wanted to chat for a while. The sun has had taken its toll on her arms and upper chest. (I was not looking at her breasts by the way.) They were wrinkled and over tanned from years spent outdoors. (Her arms, not her breasts. I'm going to stop digging.) She wore a wedding ring but was here alone. I started to wonder about her story.

"So tell me about you then?" I asked.

"Ah, me?" She hesitated for a second and dropped her head and drew a circle with her finger on the table. I knew something sad was about to come.

"Well, I recently had a car accident and my husband was killed. We never had any children and now I am travelling the world."

She wanted to get it all out in one sentence. A sentence she has clearly said many times.

"I am so, so sorry to hear that." I said nervously as I am really bad at condolences. Not another widowed women. I really know how to pick them, don't I.

"That's alright, no biggie. It's been a year now."

"So where have you been then?" I said, quickly trying to change the subject.

She seemed happy to change the conversation and started to rattle off all the interesting places she has seen. I was very jealous, although took comfort in the fact I still have 25 years to do what she has done by her age.

"Wow, I really want to go to Mongolia." I said.

"It's the best place in the world, but don't take the Trans Siberian. It's shit. Seriously mate! Four days of the same scenery and sharing a cabin with a stinking drunk Chinese businessman who seemed to have a week's worth of meetings and no shower." She laughed at her own joke. I do that. I like her already.

"The best thing is to fly to Ulan Bator or take the Trans Siberian from Beijing."

"Cool!" is all I could say. I just wanted her to carry on, but then one of the Ego Travellers butted in, trying to get the one-up on Sophie.

"I have been there too. It's awesome. Did you go to the Gobi?"

"Of course, you can't go to Mongolia and not see the Gobi," replied Sophie.

"It's awesome isn't it? Did you stay in one of those Mongolian hut things?"

"A Ger?" said Sophie.

"Yeah, a Ger. I knew it started with a G," he said.

I butted in. "So, Sophie, if you had 1 month off and £2000 to spend, what would you do?"

I always ask people this question. It's a great personality question, especially for speed dating. I can't stand people who say they would go to Tenerife and sit in the sun to get a tan. How boring.

"Easy! I would climb Uhuru." (Mt Kilimanjaro)

"No way? Me too." I said excitedly.

I was totally honest too. I would love to climb it one day. Not in the immediate future but possible when one of my children turn 16. Not that they'll be at all interested, but one can hope. (I don't even have a girlfriend yet by the way. Should probably get one first before thinking about what my imaginary kids are going to do when they are 16.)

47

"Well if you ever decide to do it, email me."
"For sure," she replied.

Sophie and I spent the next few hours chatting away. I was glad she was there and I didn't have to spend the entire evening with Ego Travellers.

Must have been midnight by the time I head up to the dorm after saying goodnight to Sophie and taking her email, promising to email when either of us decides to climb Kilimanjaro. It's dark and I can't turn the light on. This sucks! I have the top bunk near the window. A huge streetlamp lights up my whole bed. Luckily I am tired and hope to get a good sleep. I hope no one snores!

Dartmoor

Huge pork pie

Exeter to Yeovilton

They bloody snore! All of them. It was like a very bad choir. I hate hostels. Camping is the way forward from now on. People snoring, farting, talking, and worst of all, the guy on the bunk bellow must have been dreaming about Angelina Jolie all night. There was a lot of groaning!

I have to get out of here now!

I headed out early and got totally lost again but soon found the A30. It was busy but I needed to get out the city and make up for getting lost yesterday. The going was pretty flat, boring and uneventful. I soon found my mind wandering.

"Did you know cows ruled the world once," said Little Flying Cow.

"Yeah right."

"No they did. We were the supreme race. What do you think COWS stand for?"

"Creature Of Wide Steaks," I said, quite impressed by my quick wittedness.

"HAHA, very funny. It actually stands for Creators Of World Stability."

"What?"

"Yeah, before the first Ice Age, cows ruled the world. What do you think Cowboys are? They used to be our slaves. The average salary for such an honour was 2 pints of milk a

day."
Such a ridiculous idea actually started to make sense in my mind. It's amazing what goes through your mind when you spend hours and hours cycling alone. A truck zoomed past me almost blowing me over. I really must concentrate. Back to reality! I'm losing it already.

I stopped in Honiton, another 'Market Town' apparently. Cornish people love their markets they do. Can't find the market though. Turns out I'm in Devon and not Cornwall anyway which is cool. Two counties down and a bunch more to go. Told you I haven't planned much.

I am becoming addicted to coffee. It's probably the high I mistake for energy that it gives me. It's great sitting in the coffee shop observing people taking an interest in Valerie. Most see her all kitted out, then call to their partner and point. They both then look at her, then look around to see if they can see the person she belongs too. Only a few manage to clock me in the window and wave or give me the thumbs up.

One kind gentleman even gave me a bag of raisin buns. We chatted for a while and he tells me stories of when he cycled around Ireland for 3 weeks. How nice. My mood has been lifted now that I was out of a busy city and back in the countryside. As I left, he warned me about some long hills to come. No! Not hills! I can feel my legs cramping already.

1 hour later . . .

I have no idea what raisin bun man was on about. These

hills are a piece of cake. Maybe I am finally getting fit. Yay!!!

I am making such good time I decide to stop at an Air Museum in Yeovilton. It's incredible. James, (my business partner who is probably pulling all his hair out right now because I am not there to help,) would love it here. He got his pilot's licence when he was 17 or some stupidly young age like that. He is one of those guys who knows what plane is flying above just by the sound of the engine.

The museum had pretty much every plane you could imagine. They even had a Concorde. It was surprisingly small to be honest. I can't believe Pink Ties used to spend so much money on a flight they could hardly stand up in.

My favourite was the old-school helicopters. I love choppers and used to go up in them while looking for herds of elephant when I was a child. My dad's friend Vera (which means 'feathers' in Afrikaans – no wonder he became a pilot) had a few helicopters and the one we went up in the most had no doors. Vera knew how scared this made me but he still took as many sharp corners as he could. I was practically hanging by my seat belt as if it were a parachute harness. I swear they weren't designed for 7 year olds and I could have quite easily slipped through the bottom of them. You got to love 'Health & Safety', or complete lack thereof, in Africa.

After spending an hour pretending I was a fighter pilot, I decided to find the nearest campsite and make the most of the lovely evening. It's finally sunny. I can hardly control my happiness. I am feeling in the cooking mood and head off to the supermarket to get supplies for a gourmet meal. I say gourmet, but I am kind of limited to what I can cook so settle for some pasta with chopped up pepperoni, tomatoes and some sunflower seeds. I don't know why I bought the sunflower seeds. Someone mentioned they were good for the brain. As a treat, I also bought a bottle of beer. A whole 750ml of ice cold beer. What a treat!

As I only have two pots and no plate, I have to figure the best way to cook what I have bought. After at least 15 minutes of um'ing and arr'ing, I decided to just put everything I have into one of the pots and boiled it up.

After a good 30 minutes on the boil the pasta is ready. It doesn't look like much, in fact it looks more like what you see on the pavement at 3 am outside Kebab King while waiting for the 43 bus to take me home.

I put those thoughts behind me and open my beer while tucking into my gourmet meal. It's so good. I really should do this more often. It couldn't have been 30 seconds after I finished my meal when it started to bloody rain again. Seriously! This is becoming a joke. I pack up my stove and pots quickly and head down to the nearest pub. It's only 3 minutes walk but I still managed to get drenched. Not drowned rat style this time, but pretty close.

The pub was quaint like most small town pubs are. Thick stone walls with black wooden window frames and the most random stuff on the windowsill you have ever seen.

I don't think I knew what half the things were. Probably artefacts to do with mining things. That's as much as I know about this part of the world. Markets and mines.

The only thing I could recognise was one of those old-school irons that you needed to heat up on a stove while ironing. I know this because that's what we had when I was a kid. I think I still have it somewhere. It's all polished brass now as a kind of decorative display piece, much like this one in the pub, only mine was more impressive. As if irons can impress at all?

They say Guinness is a meal in a glass, so I order one as I need as many calories as possible. I have one of those stupid metabolisms whereby I need to eat half a cow with fries just to stay normal weight. My flatmate is a fitness instructor and measured my body fat before I left. I am at 12% which is 'very lean' according to the chart. Good thing I am not very tall so I don't come across as being skinny. Hopefully after a month of cycling I may bulk up a bit. Bring on toned calf muscles.

The pub is playing 'Silent Night'. That's hilarious! It's bloody April. I love it. I wonder if one of the barmen (there are only two) had a bet to play it. I would make up all sorts of things to keep my mind creative if I worked here. It's pretty quiet!

I didn't finish my Guinness because I was too full so went back to my tent. It's really cold but just then I have an ingenious plan. I brought one of those silver space blankets, (yes I brought a space blanket and not a camping mat or plate) which I opened up and put between the inner and outer layer of my tent. It damn near fits perfectly as if it was made for my tent. I jump in. It's so warm.

"What a great idea." I've just installed insulation to my tent. I'm progressing as a human. It's like I'm living proof that evolution exists. I fall asleep with a smile on my face.

The Air Museum

Making the most of a sunny evening

Yeovilton to Warminster

Guess what? It bloody rained again last night. Just when I was looking forward to nice relaxing breakfast. Who was I kidding? I can hardly move in my tent and eating breakfast needs a masters degree in contortionism.

"This is getting to be a joke Little Flying Cow."

"Yes, but it makes for better stories when you get back."

That thought, although adding some positivity to my situation, still didn't change the fact that I was cold and still wet because nothing had dried overnight. Not only is it a ball-ache to pack up in the rain, it also adds about 2 kgs to Valerie with water soaked clothes and tent.

My packing routine is pretty much waxed and I am on the road by 8.30 am. I am going to head across to Stonehenge as I have never been there before. It's quite a way off course but I am in no rush. Half the point of this trip is to see Britain and as long as I get to my train in 25 odd days time, I am happy.

The world record for doing this trip is something like 42 hours. That's just crazy! He must have had legs bigger than both mine put together.

By 10 am I am starving and stop at a roadside café for a 3-2-1. Two very friendly truckers are sitting in the corner. We discuss briefly the best things to see in the area before I tuck into my breakfast.

You can tell they frequent this café often by their body

language. I bet they sit in the same chairs every time and order the same meal. It's funny how as we get older we start to like routine. I am not a fan of routine but I guess if you find something that you like, why change it. Kind of like my 3-2-1 breakfast. Am I turning into a man? Is this trip the end of the beginning or the beginning of the middle stages of my life? I have a friend who told me a story that his dad told him when he turned 25. He said,

"Son. Your life, everyone's life, is divided into three stages. The first 25 years of your life are spent learning to walk, learning how to eat without spilling, learning not to wet your bed and learning the skills you need for your life on this earth. The second and middle 25 years are when you use all your new skills to create the best possible life for you and your family. Then there are the last 25 years. These are in essence the first 25 years in reverse. You forget how to walk, you forget how to eat and you start wetting your bed again."

Although quite hilarious, I do love the concept. I also felt that I should be a little further down the life line than I am. Maybe that philosophy was written when people died at 75. I reckon it's three sets of 30 years nowadays which is good news for me and most late 20 year olds who still haven't gotten married and had children yet. Yet another fail because I live in London. Not too stressed though. I can wait.

After my 3-2-1, I was just about to get on my bike when a bunch of students arrived at the café and, like most teenagers, were very excitable about my trip. We had a good chat. The dominant guy in the group, the one asking all the questions, looked like he was straight out of Boy-

Band School. His little head flick to get his high-lightened hair out his face was now so subconscious that he sometimes did it even though there was no hair in his eyes at all. They were all very complimentary though and I posed for a photo with all of them. We got one of the truckers to take it. I wonder where photos like that ever land up. Maybe I will be in some Facebook album with a little note below reading 'The ginger man cycling Britain with a tent.' One of them even gave me 37p. A very kind gesture, which made me smile as they all give me an over enthusiastic send off. I better not slip or fall over now. That would be embarrassing.

The map says that Stonehenge is 30 miles away and I have an awesome tail wind. The road is a bit narrow and once or twice the draught from a few trucks nearly sends me into an adjacent field.

There are two types of draughts. One is from trucks overtaking me which kind of sucks me into the road so I have to lean away in order to keep near the edge. It's a fine balancing act because as soon as the truck is past I have to correct my balance so as not to fall over into a ditch.

The second draught, and by far the worst kind, are the ones from trucks coming in the opposite direction. Unlike the overtaking draught, this one is more aggressive and it feels like you've been hit in the face with a plank of wood. Oak, not Ply!

I have learned to anticipate the draught from the oncoming trucks by taking a deep breath and puffing my chest out as if I were a chipmunk guarding his nuts. I then lean forward over Valerie's handlebars and put my head down. As the plank hits my head I let out a long growl, my face all tightened up, teeth showing. It's almost second nature now and must be quite a sight for people who see me doing it.

"I can see it in the distance, Little Flying Cow. Stonehenge." I was on a back road heading northeast towards the silhouetted rocks on the horizon. I was really excited to see something that was over 5,000 years old. My excitement now radiating into actual energy, and I started to pedal faster. As I get nearer and nearer, my excitement slowly turns to bitter disappointment. There is a main road running right next to it and to add to the completely commercialised feel, there was a huge fence surrounding it too.

"They've cocked this one up, Little Flying Cow. Seriously! I can't believe I have just used three burgers worth of precious calories to get here."

"Damn right. How awesome would the experience be if there was no road and they made you park half a mile away. You would then have to walk to it and as you walked it got bigger and bigger."

Little Flying Cow was on a rant so I let him carry on.

"It would give you the feel of what it was like 5,000 years ago to voyage to the stones for the summer solstice."

He had a point. It could have been so much better. The best thing about the whole experience was the farmer who owned the field next to Stonehenge made his own mini Stonehenge with hay bales. Now that's creativity. They should hire him for ideas.

I didn't even go into the fence and took one photo from outside then left. Crap! I am now in a bad mood and to add insult to injury I was now cycling back the way I came into a killer headwind.

My route then headed northwest through and area on the map that just said 'Danger Zone'.

"That's awesome. I wonder what the danger is? It could be huge swamplands where crocodiles and alligators live. Let's go and have a look. Come on, let's do it. It'll be fun. Come on."

"We don't have time and no, it's not swampland. We are on an open plain, it must be something else."

My sensibility was overriding Little Flying Cow's sense of adventure. Just then I heard a huge bang and nearly fell over. I stopped and looked around to see if I could see anything. My heart had practically jumped out my chest. As if it wasn't beating hard enough to start with. There was the eerie quietness you get after a big bang as even the birds stop chirping.

"OOOOh! How spooky."

I decided to look at the map again and there it was. In small print under Danger Zone were the words 'Army Training Area'. It must have been a tank or something. They really should put more warning signs here. There aren't even any fences. What if a deaf tourist decided to go for a walk one Sunday afternoon? They would just be out walking with their binoculars and the next thing you know, BOOM! Mincemeat! Health and Safety would be all over it.

The headwinds are still crazy strong, but after a long slog I finally get to Warminster. There is a great looking pub as I am entering the town so I cycle round the back and spend the normal 5 minutes chaining Valerie to a gate.

I go into the pub only to find out they don't do food anymore. What? There is even a big sign out front saying

'Food served all day'. I leave and spend another 5 minutes unchaining Valerie and head further into town.

Eventually I find a Morrison supermarket. Jackpot! They do the cheapest food ever. I chain Valerie up again and head in for the biggest meal I have had in days. I probably stink but I don't care. Food comes first. I say that a lot but somehow never learn.

As I was finishing, an old man, even older than most of the oldies, turned around from the table in front of me and started up a conversation but for the life of me I couldn't understand a word he said.

"Hay ya doon t'deh. U cim fey fer n wier u hedfin."

He was spraying biscuit all over the place because of the huge gap in his front teeth. I felt really sorry for the old man and really wanted to have a chat but really couldn't understand him. I just nodded and said I was cycling Britain for charity. He must have been asking about that. I hope so otherwise he must think I am a complete idiot. He gave me a huge wet biscuit smile. It wasn't pretty. He just smiled and nodded and turned around and carried on eating. That was that. His little bit of social interaction for the day and he was happy. What a simple life. I do wonder what he was like in his youth. Probably one of 'the lads eh'.

I finished eating and looked at my watch. It was nearly dark and I had no idea where I was staying. I ask a Policeman but he doesn't know of any campsites and I can't find any on the map.

I decide that I might have to stay in a B&B so will head out of town and stay in the first one I can find. There is only one road out of the town and not before long I find myself past all the houses and back onto the small country lane much like the one I came in on.

"We are not going to find anywhere to stay, we are not going to find anywhere to stay." Little Flying Cow always amped for landing us up in uncomfortable situations.

I hope he is wrong. There must be somewhere to stay. The miles go by and although my huge dinner restored my strength, I was starting to get very tired and cold. The sun had set and it was getting darker by the second. I really did not want to be cycling at night. I would surely be run over. I had no lights on Valerie. Again, don't judge me!

The miles keep going by and still nothing.

"Maybe I should turn back and find something in Warminster."

"Don't be stupid. Go and ask that man if we can stay in his field."

I looked to my right and see the lights of a farmhouse. Little Flying Cow had a point. I could stay in his field. Why not? Yes, let's ask. I cycled up to the door and knocked three times. I think three times is the perfect number of times to knock. Two is too impersonal and four is too aggressive.

I waited what seemed to be lifetime. I was really nervous. I don't know why? Finally, after at least 3 years, a man came to the door.

"Yes, how can I help you?"

He was a young farmer type man with a very strong Welsh accent. This made me at ease. I don't know why but I picture all Welsh people to be friendly.

"Hi, hello, I was wondering if I may bother you as to camp in your field tonight. I am cycling Britain for charity and have nowhere to stay. Look there is my bike with all my stuff on."

I really wanted to lay it on thick that I was desperate and also thought he may not believe me. I think I even turned around and let him read my vest just to prove I wasn't a robber or anything.

"Of course you can."

"Honey. Who is it?" It must have been his wife calling from the kitchen.

"A cyclist dear. He is going to camp in our field."

She came rushing through the door as if she hadn't quite heard right.

"This young man is cycling all of Britain for charity and needs a place to camp so he is going to camp in our field."

"Really? Ok! You are mad but OK. If you need any milk, do let us know."

"Thank you so much. You are very kind."

"Anytime," they both answered.

How friendly. Also, why is milk the one thing everyone offers? I'd prefer a steak or a beer please!

After a few more pleasantries, I said good night and headed up to the field. I could see that the couple were quite chuffed they had a charity cyclist in their field.

The field is at a slope overlooking the Wiltshire countryside. Ah! I'm in Wiltshire. Turns out I went through Somerset too and didn't realise. I set up my tent near the bottom of the slope. It is much less steep and the grass is much thicker which will make for a comfortable night.

"I could kill for a beer now, Little Flying Cow."

"I think I saw a pub half a mile back. It looked a bit rough, but a beer is a beer eh!"

True to form there was a pub down the road and even more true was its roughness. This pub has certainly seen its fair share of brawls. There is a football match on, and as I am a rugby and cricket man I order probably the best lager in the world, and sit quietly at a table near some equally uninterested-in-football kids playing tennis on a Nintendo Wii. What an invention Wii tennis is. I have broken many a light shade trying to mimic a Pete Sampras serve in my mate Matt's lounge after a few too many beers. Matt? Wasn't he responsible for my leaving drinks hangover? Ah! He was blatantly getting me back for all the broken lampshades.

"Well hello there sir, I haven't seen you here before."

I turn to the seat next to me where a man who has obviously spent too long in the pub is sitting and smiling at me.

"No you haven't. I am just passing through. I am busy being an idiot and cycling Britain."

"Really? Why would you want to do that? That's a stupid idea."

"I don't think so. It's a great way to see the countryside and raise money for charity."

"Charity-shmarity, they don't need the money. Trust me. Keep it for yourself." He was stuttering over his words. He also had most of the buttons of his salmon shirt undone revealing a tacky gold chain and a blindingly white potbelly. He must have been in his mid fifties.

"I think we should all do our bit for charity. Don't you?"

"Ha," he let out one laugh and I knew a wave of opinion was about to ensue. "Let me tell you something son. When I was your age I was a millionaire. This was back in the 70's when Britain used to export fish to Europe rather than the other way round. I made my first million by the age of 22 and gave loads of money to charity. Then my life turned upside down. The industry changed and Spain and France didn't want my fish anymore. I lost everything and to top it all off, I realised I was gay so lost my family too. Now I am here almost every night getting drunk."

He put his hand on my leg. I felt a little awkward as I am not good with touchy-feely people, especially drunk old gay men looking for some action – probably.

"So you see. I gave to charity but when I needed a helping hand do you think there was anyone to help me? No, is the answer. No! What are you drinking?"

He got up and hobbled over to the bar before I could answer. I was glad he wasn't touching my leg anymore. When he reached the bar and looked back questioningly. "So?"

"Lager please, thank you, Carlsberg."

"Probably the best lager in the world, hey kid."

He stumbled back spilling half of my beer on the already beer ridden carpet. "Oops!" He laughed as if he does it all the time as he sat down next to me.

"My name is Pete," he said after taking a huge gulp of beer.

"Nice to meet you Pete, I am Conners."

We shook hands and I think I may have broken his fingers. We just didn't make a good connection because he chose to wimp out of a real hand-shake. I hate that.

"So I take it you don't like football then?" I asked.

"Nah! Useless game. In fact most sport is useless. What's the point? Just a bunch of people running around chasing some sort of ball. Blah! There's only one set of balls I like, if you know what I mean?"

Okay! I didn't know how to react so just laughed with my nervous fake laugh and caught my head nodding. That's how you tell when I fake laugh. My head nods. Thinking about my fake laugh downfall actually made me laugh properly so I don't think he noticed.

There was an awkward silence for a while. I am usually not bothered with awkward silences but Pete felt the need to keep me company so shouted out.

"Ben, Ben, leave that game and come here. Ben!"

A young and very drunk guy came stumbling over with a smile. He must have just turned 18 and didn't quite know how to handle his drink.

"What ya want, you gay drunk?" he laughed jokingly.

"This is Conners, he is cycling the whole of Britain for charity. Give him some money, will you."

He turned and looked at me then brought his face to within 15cm of mine. "Na way. That's awesome. Here's a quid."

He took my hand to shake it while getting a quid from his pocket with the other. His face was still 15cm from mine, his breath smelt awful.

"Thanks mate. That's very kind of you."

"Leave this old fart alone and come sit with us over there."

He pointed to a bunch of his mates watching football.

It's weird. Although Pete was clearly pissed and talking nonsense, I kind of felt sorry for him. I mean, he has had quite a life and he did just buy me a beer. I couldn't just get up and leave.

"Let me just finish my beer and I'll be over."

He just smiled and sort of wafted around and went back to his mates. Pete and I sat and chatted while we both had another beer before he got up and bid me farewell, claiming he had to get up at 5 am for his security guard shift. There was no way he was going to make it. I actually laughed for real when he said it. He laughed back and as he left he gave me £20.

"I hate charities but you seem like a decent fellow so here, go save the planet or something."

I was shocked. Such a nice guy. To hate something but still see the bigger picture was such a good trait. Pete left and I was in the mood for another beer so went over to sit with Ben and the last of his group of mates. The football was now over and most of them had gone home.

"Oi! Cycle man. How's it going? Beer?"

He rushed up to the bar and much like Pete earlier I had to shout my order from my chair. Also like Pete he managed to spill half of it on the floor. I laughed to myself. I was in a good mood.

"So this cycle trip, you are a mad man?"

"I know, I know," I said.

Just then his mate jumped in. "Hi I'm Chris. That's just brilliant mate. Where have you come from? Where are you going?"

He was really interested in my trip.

"Stonehenge this afternoon but I thought it was rubbish."

"Yeah I know! It's not what it used to be like. I remember when me and my dad used to go there as a kid. You could walk all around them stones and touch them and stuff. I remember even scratching my name in one of them."

I nearly choked on my beer. What an idiot. It's people like him that has made it like it is today. He continued.

"It's just not the same anymore. It's like a prison. It really is. It's a prison."

Although I didn't agree with his first statement and not wanting to cause another pub brawl, I went along with the prison idea and agreed. I looked over at Ben to see his opinion but he was fast asleep.

"Bloody Ben right. He always falls asleep. Kids can't take their drink nowadays. Not like when we were lads like," laughed Chris, then turning back to me asked. "So where you staying tonight? I have a spare bedroom if you need. Honest I do. It's no bother."

"Thanks anyway but I am camped up down the road."

"Well you pop in in the morning for a shower and breakfast if you like. No.75. Just turn right out here and first left. No. 75. The red door."

People are so friendly out here and although I didn't agree with Chris's nonchalant views on vandalism, he was still a sound guy.

I didn't stay much longer in the pub as I knew I would already be feeling the beer in the morning. I hate how the fitter you get the more of a lightweight you become. The half mile walk back to my field was in pitch darkness and I practically had to dive into the hedgerow whenever a car came by.

Stonehenge (looks better in photos)

Camping in a farmer's field

Warminster to Bath

I had the best sleep ever which was probably due to the 4 beers I had in the pub last night. I also remember having an awesome dream, although I can't remember what it was about. I wish I could because it really was a good one. It's 7.30 am and it's NOT raining. I am heading to the Fox-Talbot Museum. This man practically invented my career, photography, and invented the positive negative system which allowed us to reproduce the same image over and over again. I can't wait to get there, so head off early.

The museum is in a town called Lacock and after making the mistake of pronouncing it like I was French (La'Cock) was soon corrected to the actual pronunciation which is *Lay-cock*. I think La'Cock is way better though. It's a quaint little town. Probably the best town I have been to in England. It used to be an old cotton & wool trading town but now is a picture postcard British village that attracts many tourists to its miniature streets and very small doorways.

I've always wondered why old doorways are small. Were people smaller or trees shorter? Who knows? I could picture myself living here when I am an old man. I would spend my days walking the streets with my wife as we take in the afternoon's sun. In the winter I would make ginger cider (the root and not bits of my hair) and my wife would bake bread. Everyone would love my cider and my wife's bread, so much so we would start selling it in the local shop.

I would only be able to make a few bottles a week though for my passion would still be photography. My cottage would be covered with photographs that I had taken throughout my career and I would take pride in the photo I took of Prince William back in 2006. (This is actually true. I have photographed Will, as I like to call him now. Ha. Kidding. He doesn't reply to my letters either...) He would be The King of England by then and it would be my *thing,* my story that I told whenever I met people, even though they have all heard it a thousand times before.

The museum was brilliant and I spend hours just wandering the grounds of the huge manor house that Fox-Talbot lived in. Man, he was loaded. That I didn't know. I stood where he stood when taking some of those first photos of the women below the bay window. I took the exact same photo too but without the Victorian dressed women of course. I felt inspired.

The photography industry can be tough at times and it's always good to get back to your roots now and again. I read the visitor's books and laughed at all the comments made by what must have been teenage kids dragged there by their parents. One read: 'Very, very boring. All the photos are blurred. My 3 year old sister Abby takes better photos and she is rubbish. I wish I had stayed at home – Sam'. She or he (I never know with the name Sam) just didn't get it. So sad.

After the Museum, I start heading out of town. I walk past an old man. He must be in his 90's and looking very dapper. Full suit, including waistcoat, top-hat and wooden cane.

"Excuse me young man, can I give you some money for your charity?" He hands out a fiver and has a huge smile on his face.

"Of course sir, thank you very much."

"It's OK," he paused briefly. "Could I have £4 change please?"

Brilliant. He wanted to give me a quid but only had a note. Most people wouldn't bother but he went through with it. I loved that. I gave him £4, said thanks and went to find Valerie.

My morning of exploring Talbot Manor and meeting old English folk has put me in the Cream Tea mood so went off to find a small tearoom. It wasn't hard. The best one was situated in an old stone house with windows that distort your view because they were made with a hammer – probably.

I went in and definitely stood out from the crowd. The tearoom was full of older couples dressed much like the man who gave me a quid. Dapper and proper, reading the Guardian and doing crosswords that might as well be in Gaelic they are so hard. I, in my fluorescent jacket and smelling like last week's rugby socks, didn't quite add to the atmosphere. I'm surprised they let me stay. I'm glad they did because the Cream Tea was the best I've ever had. Although that doesn't say much because I think I've only ever had Cream Tea 3 times. I normally always run out of cream, or jam, and have to eat the last half scone dry, but not here. They pilled it on thick. Happy me!

My journey from here is pretty easy until I reach Bath tonight where I am actually going to have a bed for the first time.

My friend Helen lives there and has offered me a place to stay. I think it may even be downhill the whole way. I hope so. I could do with a rest on the knees. Although I have been to Bath before, I am looking forward to it anyway. I love all the old streets. I don't even know what day it is now and that's the way I like it. I feel free and in control of my adventure. Finally!

"We can do whatever we want to, can't we Little Flying Cow?"

"This is true. We can do anything. How about we win the lottery? What would you do with the money?"

"Easy! I would buy my parents a house each and pay off all their debt. Then I would throw a massive party for all my friends and then go and travel to all the places Australian Sophie had been to and more. How about you? What would you do with millions?"

I started to think what would happen if a millionaire left all his fortune to a cow. People have done that in the past to dogs. Left them millions. I really can't see the point in that. Seriously! Dogs lick their own arses.

"I would convert everyone to vegetarians, except they can eat goats and sheep, them lot are weird. Cows ruled the world, remember. I would then buy the biggest paddock in all of Gloucestershire and get myself 100 of the fattest wives known to cows. We are allowed many wives. It's the best thing about being a cow."

I'm officially going mad.

The final section into Bath is a long and steady downhill. I don't think I peddled for 20 minutes. I just put my head down and listened to the rush of the wind fly past my ears. Every now and then I would close my eyes for a few seconds and pretend I was in a fighter jet. The sound of my wheels on the tar road mimicked its jet engine and the wind going past me made me feel as if I were going supersonic. I love imagining myself in a whole new world for just a split second. It keeps my mind busy which is very important so as not to go mad. Or is it in fact the beginning of madness?

By the time I reach Bath I can hardly feel my hands or feet. The temperature dropped the lower down the valley I went and the wind cut through my gloves and shoes like razor blades. I love Bath. Every street looks a thousand years old. Bath has *actual* baths too. Roman ones. I've never been to them but hope to one day. I'll just have to settle for a modern bath at Helen's.

I made my way to Helen's house and knocked on the door. I had to knock twice because I wasn't sure I actually connected with the door the first time. Hands have lost all feeling. I heard someone running down some stairs and then the door flew open and there stood Helen with the most welcoming face I've ever seen.

"Dude, I can't believe you've cycled all the way from Cornwall. That's awesome."

I try and talk but I can't even move my lower jaw and have to wait a good 5 minutes to thaw out before I can speak without drooling or sounding drunk. Helen is always happy. Probably the happiest person I know which is why she is awesome to hang around.

"Yeah, it's been amazing. The best adventure so far. I can't believe I've still got like 3 more weeks of it."

I retold Helen of all the fun places I'd seen, the people I'd met and the rain I've had to endure. I practically didn't stop talking for hours. It's nice to tell stories to people you know. I was definitely making up for a week spent practically alone. Luckily Helen was really interested. (Or is good at pretending.) Some of my other friends might have faked an 'important' phone call - like you get on first dates.

"I have an early birthday present for you."

She gives me a present. It's my birthday in a few days time. What a legend. I open my present. It's a pair of proper posh cycling socks. I've finally been upgraded to a real cyclist. I really needed them, as my current pair weren't doing so well. I had kind of forgotten it was my birthday, so the fact the Helen remembered was pretty impressive.

"I have something else for you. Wait here."

In a flash, she disappeared out of the lounge. What could it be? I was still all excited about trying my new posh socks. Moments later I hear Helen singing.

"Happy Birthday to you . . . ."

She walks in with the best looking cake in the world.

"No way. Thank you so much. I never get cakes."

"Thought you might need the calories."

I cut the cake, made a wish and tucked it.

"This is the best cake I have ever had."

I wasn't lying. My extreme hunger may have had something to do with it but it was amazing.

The evening continued with laughs, food, cake and beer. A definite psychological boost to what's been a rainy few days. The last thing I remember is trying to work out why my duvet was lighting up the living room. Turns out Helen has a glow-in-the-dark spare duvet cover. I don't know what Helen's main duvet is but it must be pretty cool if this is the spare one.

Fox Talbot Museum

Helen the legend

Bath to Cheltenham

After sleeping on a good bed, I realise I need a new tent and a camping mattress. I don't care if a bigger tent adds two whole days to my trip because of the extra weight. I just need to be able to sit up straight and have a place to put my stinking bloody clothes where I won't suffocate from the fumes.

I am angry at how I didn't think this through properly before I left. My neck and back are stiff and tight, and my sleeping bag stinks from the dirty clothes-mattress I make each night when the ground is hard. At least the rain has stopped, even though it is very overcast. My next stop is Cheltenham and there must be a camping store there. It's only about 4 hours cycle away, I think, which will give me enough time to shop around when I get there.

I say goodbye to Helen and have some more of the amazing cake she got me. Yes. I had cake for breakfast. I'm so rock and roll right now. She also made me a pack lunch. What a legend. Not to mention I am wearing my new dry, comfortable socks. Wiggo beware! I've got new socks!

The hill out of Bath is a killer and my legs and neck are burning. I have to stop and have a banana half way up before carrying on the struggle. As I get higher and higher, the fog sets in and soon I can't see more than 20 metres in front of me. Huge trucks can't see me either and have to swerve at the last minute so as not to run me over.

"This is dangerous stuff, hey! Good one for the Blog." Little Flying Cow always looking for the positive things. I wasn't in the mood and after 3 near death collisions with trucks, I am forced to ride on the very thin pavement. It's no more than 15cm wide and covered in moss, bumps and pieces of glass. The chance of getting a puncture is about 6543% higher. My handlebars are now also about 5cm away from the barrier on the edge of the road. If I clip the edge then I'll surely be flung off Valerie like that time I went on a bucking bronco.

The going is pretty slow and wet. Not only are my legs burning, but my mind is now tired from having to concentrate so hard on where I am going. If I lose concentration, I may slip off the thin slippery pavement and Valerie and I would surely fall right into the middle of the road where we would be run over by a truck who would probably not even realise he had run us over either. We would both then be run over, over and over again as no one else would see us through the fog until there is nothing left of us. What a horrible thought but then again, I was in a horrible mood. Oh, and to add to it all my new dry socks were soaking wet. Not happy!

The fog didn't ease up at all for about 2 hours and by now I was truly soaked to the bone. The only comfort I got was the knowledge that tonight, for the first time I may be able to relax properly in a new larger tent. That kept me going. It's the small things that count.

I arrive in Cheltenham at around 1 pm and head straight for the centre of town. Cheltenham is a great little town with everything you need. I soon find a popular outdoor shop and set to work looking for a decent 2-man tent. This is also the first time I have been in large crowds since Paddington at the beginning of the trip. A few people chat to me, which is nice but I think I must really smell bad because they don't hang around for long.

Finally, I find what I am looking for. A beautiful, fairly light, 2 man tent with a porch area to keep my clothes dry and cook under. It's the Titanic of two man tents. I fell in love with it the minute I turned to its page. It's olive green and shaped like a tunnel, which makes it perfect for the windy nights ahead. It is four times the price of my current tent but it's a small price to pay for my sanity.

The rest of the afternoon is taken up by finding a post office to post my other tent home and then grabbing a cheap pub meal. Tomorrow is my birthday so I find a small bakery and buy a tiny cake. Everyone has to have a cake on their actual birthday. I felt a little greedy because I'd had a cake already but convinced myself I needed the calories. I thought of getting a candle but I didn't fancy burning down my new highly flammable tent on its inaugural night out.

Damn it. Why did I say *Titanic* and *Inaugural* when referring to my tent? I'm doomed.

Being in the Cotswolds, I thought it would be a good idea to find a picturesque campsite overlooking the beautiful rolling countryside that surrounds Cheltenham. I am spoiled for choice in this part of the world and it's a pretty certain bet they will be empty too. I head northwest out of the city. I have decided to cycle along the Welsh borders so as to miss out Birmingham. I really don't want to land up in another ruddy Backpackers or Youth Hostel.

A few hours later, I find a very beautiful campsite. It's a small one, which seems to be in someone's field behind their house. I prefer these ones. They are a lot more personal than the big ones that take caravans.

I am met by a lovely old lady. She was putting up her washing when I came around the corner and I damn near scared the living socks off her. Bless her. At least I might have had more socks if that had actually happened. Dry ones too.

"You look like you could do with a nice cup of tea," she offered.

"Oh. You read my mind. Thank you so much. Milk and one, no make it two sugars."

I really need the energy so am trying to eat as much chocolate and sugar as I can.

"One cuppa coming right up. You can set up over there if you want, just don't go too near the lake as we have a new goose with a nest and we don't want to chase her away."

"No problem, I will just set up near the hedge."

I pointed away from the goose nest. The lady seemed pleased with my choice as she shuffled off to her house. I was really looking forward to setting up my new tent. It was like it was my birthday or something; well actually it almost was, so I let myself get into the happy mood that birthdays still bring me. I am not looking forward to the days when birthdays don't excite me anymore. I hope that never happens.

All the hardship from yesterday and this morning have almost disappeared as I sit in the afternoon light, drinking a nice cup of tea and unpacking my things. It is quite cold this evening with a slight wind coming in from the northeast but the hedge keeps me sheltered. I am the master in the art of 'tent placement'. In fact if there were a degree, I would get a first. What am I saying? It's not rocket science. Need to sleep!

My new tent is a palace. So streamlined and sleek on the outside. The wind whips over it without even making the fabric move. The ropes are stretched so tight you could play a tune on them and the ground is perfect for tent pegs; not too hard and not too muddy. Then there is the inside. The zip in the front opens into a huge porch area. It's probably as big as the whole of my other tent. From the porch is another half circle zip leading inside.

It's so big I don't know where to put everything. I still haven't decided on my unpacking strategy but for now I am sleeping down the right hand side with my clothes at the bottom and my maps and cameras down the left hand side. The porch area has all my food and wet clothes.

"Now this we could get used to, Little Flying Cow. Look how big it is."

"Hell yeah. We could be on MTV Cribs."

I put on a fake American accent.

"Hi, I am Conners cycling Britain and this is my crib. Now over here we have the patio and as you can see the wonderful views. These views are so spectacular; they change every single day. The patio then leads onto my double bedroom which has been decorated with the best furnishings that can be found. (I could afford.) Don't you just love the way the bed runs beautifully down the right - it's so feng-shui. Now let's take a look at my wheels. Here I have the latest Dawes Horizon. This baby is the Mustang of the cycling world and gets from 0 – 15mph in under 10

seconds. (On a downhill with a tailwind.) Amazing! Let's not forget the personal entertainment system I had installed. It's called The Little Flying Cow. It's top of the range."
I was really getting carried away until I heard the little old lady coming. I started to whistle and sing as if that's all I was doing all along. I think I got away with it. She just came over to wish me luck and say that I didn't need to pay for my stay. How nice. The generosity of people continually gives me new hope in the human race.

My unpacking is followed by the best shower I have had in my entire life. Honestly, how can a simple invention like the shower bring so much pleasure? I let the perfectly pressured water run down my face and onto the back of my neck. I keep my eyes closed and listen to the water trickle down my ears. Small goosebumps appear every time I expose the back of my neck to the slight breeze coming in from the window above. I don't know how long I showered for but by the time I finished, it was dark outside. I also take the opportunity to wash all my clothes. I am on the inside-out, back-to-front day on one pair of underpants. One more day and I would have had to bin them, I think. There would be no way of saving those bad boys. I don't have any soap but rigorously thrashing them around in the water certainly gets all the sweat out. At least that's what I convince myself is happening. It probably just spreads out the smell. Oh well!

The wind starts to pick up so I settle into my tent for the evening. I still can't get over how much room I have. I even have space to boil water for my morning coffee. On the subject of boiling, I am boiling up some pasta for dinner. It's just one of those cheap packet pasta meals. Probably not the healthiest but I need to be less reckless with eating out because my new tent has made a huge dent in my budget.

A little bit misty outside Bath

First night in new tent

Cheltenham

I wake up at 7 am and instantly remember it's my birthday. I hum 'happy birthday' to myself and smile while doing so. I also notice how dark it is. This tent really does keep the morning light out.

It's bloody freezing, so much so I can't even get out of my sleeping bag. I don't mind though. I think I may take the day off and stay here another night. Lying in my tent, I listen to all the different sounds of the morning. The birds start chirping and I wonder what they are saying to each other. I wonder if there is one bird that always gets up too early and gets told by the other birds to keep it down. Can birds inter-communicate between species?

I have always wanted to come back in another life as a bird, although it's not my favourite reincarnation creature of choice. I would love to be a dolphin, shark, or any underwater fish. That's also my favourite dream, the dream where I can breathe underwater. I prefer it to flying. I don't know why. My mum always said I was a water baby, whatever that means.

It must be near 9 am when I eventually decide to venture outside. I undo the zip and look outside. Holy crap. The field, my tent, Valerie, Little Flying Cow and everything is covered in snow. 3 inches of the stuff. No wonder my tent was so dark.

I wipe the snow off Little Flying Cow's face. He is stone

cold frozen, poor thing. I can't believe it has snowed in April, and on my birthday. I am trying to work out whether this is a good thing or a bad thing.

On the one side being an African kid, snow still has a mystic childish appeal, but on the other side I am worried that the weather is going to be awful for the rest of the trip. Last year I swam in Brighton on my birthday. It wasn't completely by choice though. A drunken game of Frisbee near the water was always going to result in a wayward throw going 20 metres in. As it was my birthday, there seemed to be unanimous decision that I should go and fetch it. I stripped down to my underwear and dived in.

The shock of the cold water practically paralyzed me. I spluttered about trying to get the Frisbee and after finding it, then had the painful task of stumbling on the pebbled beach trying to get out the water. On exiting the water I notice parents turning their kids' faces away from me and covering their eyes. Other people were laughing too. I looked down to realise my underwear was completely see-through and Little Johnny, who was now seriously little, was on full show.

Luckily I had the Frisbee and managed to cover myself while a mate went and got me a towel. He took his time though. Bastard! It was quite funny actually when I look back on it. That was 12 months ago exactly and now it's snowing. What's this global warming malarky?

If this snow has brought one thing, it's that I am definitely not cycling anywhere today. I am ahead of schedule and quite fancy a day just wandering the countryside. First things first though. Cake time! I jump back into my tent so excitedly I kick a bunch of snow straight into my sleeping bag. Calm down Duracell, I think to myself while remembering the nickname I had at school. It had dual meaning. I was really hyperactive with everlasting energy, and I also have a copper top (ginger hair) just like a Duracell battery. Kids can be creative when they want to. I actually didn't mind the nickname at all. At least I wasn't Tomato Boy like Jules who had a permanently red face, poor kid.

I rearranged my tent in preparation for a nice relaxing cup of tea and cake. The water is boiling and as I unwrap my cake from its packet, I feel an overwhelming sense of nostalgia and for the first time, loneliness. I am usually very social. You have to be when you are a photographer. Being shy doesn't go with the job description. Unless you photograph shampoo bottles, I guess. Life in London is stressful and busy, and although I work from home, I do mix with many different people all the time, constantly meeting new clients, models, make-up artists, and so on. I think this is the first time I've spent more than a few days alone for a while. I've loved it up to right this second but spending my birthday alone does make me wish for company, even if just for today.

By the time the water had boiled, the first sip of tea seemed to bring a new wave of relaxation over me. There was no point in feeling lonely. I tucked into my lemon cheesecake and let my mind wander. I don't know how long I just sat there but by the time my tea was cold and cake was finished, I felt better. I was over the brief wave of solitude depression and ready to explore again.
"Boo-hoo. Did you cry a little? You are such a pansy."

Little Flying Cow doesn't miss a thing.

"No. I just had something in my eye. You haven't even wished me happy birthday."

"Cry baby, cry baby!"

"Don't make me leave you in the snow."

The rest of the day was spent just as I had planned. I walked as far as I could in one direction until I could go no further. I then turned around and did the exact same thing in the opposite direction. I repeated this in five different directions and everywhere I went had its own uniqueness. I took more photos that morning than I had the entire ride so far. You can't really go wrong when everything is covered in snow. Even the dullest of gate hinges becomes a piece of art when covered in snow.

Lunch was spent in a local pub. I overdosed with carbohydrates and protein and treated myself to a few pints of Guinness. My body really needs a rest and I can feel my legs getting stronger. It's brilliant how a small bit of snow puts everyone in a better mood. I find out that it is Sunday which makes sense because there are way too many kids out of school for a weekday.

Saying that, Britain is great at completely shutting down at the first sign of a little snow. That always cracks me up. 3 inches of snow and all you hear about on the News is train closures here, school closures there and the obligatory random story; *'Man survives sub zero night in car covered in snow to get to his daughters play'*. What he doesn't know is that his daughter's school is closed because of the snow and the play has been postponed until next week. The whole country forgets about wars, poverty and murderers on trial because 3 Robins died due to the tree they roosted in not having enough leaves to shelter them. I often wonder what the News Channels were going to write about if it hadn't snowed.

After a much extended lunch, I head back to my tent. I didn't want to touch the tent this morning when it was covered in snow because I was told once that, if frozen, the nylon can sometimes tear as you break the ice covering it. I don't quite know whether that is true or not, but I wasn't going to take the risk with the Titanic of tents. That's just tempting fate.

There is just enough snow left in the shadows of the hedge surrounding the field to make a 1 foot snowman. It takes me all of 5 minutes to construct, what I think to be, a very proportioned snowman. I make him thin as opposed to the big-bellied snowmen most people make. His eyes are made of small round stones from the driveway and instead of a carrot for a nose, I use a leaf folded in half and then arched to look like a nose. I call him Little Standing Snowman. Very creative, I know! Maybe he will have a chat with Little Flying Cow tonight.

By late afternoon most of the snow has melted on the tent and unless it snows tonight, should be all gone by the morning.

Dinner is a warm mug of cuppa-soup followed by another awesome shower. It can't be later than 7 pm when I tuck myself into bed and fall fast asleep to the sound of nothingness. Happy Birthday to me!

Snow on my birthday

My tidy porch area – don't judge me

Cheltenham to Mortimer's Cross

It's really cold when I wake up, but I have had a good sleep and ready to take on the next leg of my ride. My rest day has completely restored my strength. So much so I might have to have another one next week.

I head off towards the Welsh border as I want to be as far away from cycling anywhere near Birmingham as possible. The whole idea of cycling through another version of 'The Smog' actually gives me panic attacks. It's not that I am nervous about cycling in a city. I am pretty confident on the road now. It's just the whole reason for getting on Valerie for a whole month was to get away from the hustle and bustle of city life and explore the countryside. My detour north-westwards is going to add almost a day to my route, but I don't care. I still have time on my side, even after a day of rest.

All the snow from the day before had disappeared, but there was still a piercing chill in the morning air. The sun was low and not helping in any way to bring some much needed warmth. Although the scenery is beautiful, it becomes rather repetitive. At least there aren't too many hills and I seem to be eating up the miles.

My mind wanders all over the place, this time to my days at school. An all-boys school (probably explains why I am so useless at talking to girls) of 500 kids set on a farm in the middle of nowhere meant we made the most of being kids. There was none of this 'growing up too early' nonsense and every moment we weren't studying or playing sport (which was compulsory three times a week) we would play king stingers, climb trees or play practical jokes on each other.

It was at school that I also learned photography. I am not sure when exactly my photography went from being a hobby to a career but I always seem to remember making a little money on the sideline right from the beginning. Even at school, I used to photograph all the kids playing rugby and then sell them the photos. When I finished school, there was a photography prize named after me for the best photographer each year. The Sean Conway Photography Award. How funny. Apparently I got the highest mark for photography that anyone has ever achieved - a record I still hold to this day. I think I got something silly like 95%.

Yes, this is me bragging. My teacher nearly killed me when I asked her to explain what was 5% wrong with my exhibition. I thought it was a valid question but she just told me to shut up, be happy with 95% and get out of her classroom because she was busy marking other papers. I would love to go back and hand my trophy to the winner one year and give a speech about photography as a career.

"Hey Little Flying Cow, that would be a good thing to do, right?"

I started to recite what I might say. I even started to get really nervous thinking about standing in front of all those kids.

"You are rubbish, get a real job." says Little Flying Cow as if he were the crowd.

"Shut up or I will throw you in a ditch, again."
On that thought a huge truck damn near blows me right off the road. This daydreaming and talking to a toy thing is pretty dangerous. I really need to keep my mind on the road.

This section of the road has loads of badly placed drains every 100 metres or so. What a design flaw. I am going to find the man who made this road and write him a letter. Each drain is about 2 inches below the level of the road and is slap bang in the middle of where I need to cycle. To avoid them, I have to go into the road where I might be run over. Every time I ride through one, I can hear Valerie screaming as one of her spokes are about to break. They really need to make these things more bike-friendly. Every time I have to cycle in the road, I feel really bad for the truck drivers coming up behind me. You can hear them changing down at least 102 gears before they can see if it's OK to pass. Then it's up all 102 gears again to reach the speed they were travelling at. They must hate me.

By early afternoon I reach Leominster and settle into a pub for some good old-fashioned Bangers and Mash. Apparently you pronounce it *Lem-ster.* The town, not the food. Got that wrong to the annoyance of the proud local barman. Leominster is also, surprise, surprise, a market town. Are all small towns in the UK market towns? Seems like it. Not complaining though. They are all beautiful.

The pub is much like any other pub, except for the fact there are no women in it. There are random bunches of men all over the place, but no women. I have seen pubs that have mainly men, but there is always one token woman who has been dragged there by her husband or trying to get away from the kids for the afternoon. The other strange thing was that most of the men had moustaches. Have I gone back to the 70's? It's uncanny. Maybe that's why there are no women, I chuckle to myself.

My meal arrives and the smell of the food sends a few glances my way. It's funny how whenever you see food being delivered in a pub you follow the bartender to see who ordered it. (No? Just me.) It's like looking into other people's shopping trolleys at the supermarket.

I am most definitely the youngest person in the pub and you can tell people are wondering what I am up to. Probably should take my helmet off really. I forget it's there sometimes. One old man from a far table gets up and starts to head over. I have at least 20 seconds to prepare as he dodges other chairs and tables on his way over. He seems rather friendly and has the biggest moustache out of everyone in the pub. I think he even waxes the thing. His blue overshirt is slightly faded and his jeans are way too tight for him. You could tell he was a smoker because the tips of his moustache were stained yellow, as were the ends of his fingers.

"Hello there. What you like doing like over this end of the wood like?"

Brilliant, I have to have a conversation with someone who says the word 'like' 38 times a sentence.

"Hi, I am cycling Britain for Charity and stocking up on my carbohydrates," I replied pointing to my food.

"Oh, that's like brilliant like. Which way are you like heading like? Aren't you like a bit out of your way like?"

I almost didn't hear what he asked as I was trying to count

the number of times he used the word 'like'. 65 I think.

"Um, I am heading to Scotland and trying to bypass Birmingham so that's why I am here . . . like."

I just had to put a 'like' in there. Just to humour myself. He didn't seem to notice.

"Oh yes, Birmingham is a dump like. I never go there like," he says, shaking his head two or three times longer than he needed too.

"Where is a good place to camp near here?" I asked him with a mouth full of mash to avoid the awkward silence.

"Oh, when I was a kid like, me and my dad used to like go to this Abbey like not far from here like. What was it called? Oh heck, I can't remember like but if you head out on the main road like, you will see a sign for it like. It can't be more that 5 miles from here like and I believe there is a campsite near it like."

"Brilliant, I will be sure to look out for it."

"I highly recommend it like. Have a safe ride like and don't get run over like."

"Oh, I won't. These fluorescent vests are a lifesaver."

With that he nodded, smiled and headed back to his table. His friends all smiled and glanced over to him when he returned. I guess they were asking him what I was up to. I hope he came up with a better story like I'm James Bond on a secret mission undercover as a cyclist.

After lunch, I head out in the direction moustache man told me to go. The Abbey should be a nice place to camp. I cycle and cycle, but see no signs for any Abbey.

Eventually after 15 miles or so I figure I must have taken the wrong road and give up on the idea of camping at the Abbey. I look on the map, which is now falling apart because of all the rain, to find the nearest campsite. There is one about 15 miles from here. It's a bit further than I had expected to camp but it's so flat here I should make it in time. I put my head down and step it up a gear.

My legs are burning a little but I am feeling strong after my meal. I have never felt how food can affect your performance so much as I have done these last few days. I know it's obvious but I can feel a noticeable difference in my strength after a meal. I am still eating about 5 Mars Bars a day for energy. What a lifesaver. In fact in the lifesaving importance list, I would say Mars Bars are higher than my fluorescent vest. Only by a bit though. Oh, and coffee!

I think I must have been about 5 miles from the campsite when the weather took a sudden turn for the worse. The dark ominous clouds that have been brewing all day have decided to let rip. The wind picked up and as I was beginning to prepare for rain. I felt a sharp small bite in the back of my neck?

"What the flying cow was that?"

Then another one, and another. and before I knew it I was getting pelted by shotgun-pellet sized hailstones. Each hailstone felt like a small bullet piercing the back of my neck and forearms. The sounds of them bouncing off my helmet reverberated around my head with deafening consequences. I could hardly hear myself think. I closed my eyes for a second and I was in a war zone with machine gun fire all around.

"Come on, Little Flying Cow, let's cycle for cover. Come on!"

"Ha-ha. I can't feel a thing. Serves you right for leaving me in the snow the other day."
It was as if he was laughing at me. In fact, he had a constant smirk that was starting to annoy me whenever the going was getting tough. I looked ahead to see if there was anywhere to hide, but all I could see was a long narrow straight road running through open fields.

There is no hope. I have to bear with it and keep going. The harder I cycle, the quicker I will get to the campsite. I tried this theory but the harder I cycled, the harder the hailstones hit me too. I was in a no-win situation.

With the hailstones came the cold rain too and now my feet and hands were going numb. My feet have been in a constant state of numbness for most of this trip. I think this is because most of my blood is going to my legs, but now they are really numb. I think I could stick a nail through them and I wouldn't feel it. The thought of that made me flinch causing me to do a slight speed wobble. I must get to the campsite soon. It's not far now. I kept repeating that phrase until I saw the sign ahead of me.

It's crazy how when you know you are near the end you feel your body almost giving up. Like when marathon runners collapse on the finish line. Would they have collapsed if they moved the finish line 50 metres further? I don't think so. It shows how important a role the mind plays in doing a physical challenge.

I feel the same now. As soon as I saw the sign for the campsite my head started to lower and I dropped at least 5 gears. My hunched up shoulders became tight, heavy, and cold from rainwater running down the back of my neck. I stared to sing in my head – *I have cycled 500 miles and I will cycle 500 more. Just to be the man who cycle 1000 miles in all this weather of poor.* X-Factor here I come.

Another empty campsite, and another rainy evening. It's become a way of life for me now. There is no point in getting annoyed with something you can't change. Much like being ginger. Ha. Oh, the years of childhood torture rearing its nasty head again. Its ginger head at that. OK, I'll stop now!

Setting up my tent has become second nature. Although I am freezing cold, I work in autopilot putting poles here, pegs there and pulling ropes. I don't even have to think about where everything goes. I have developed a system and it works so why change it. I sound like my business adviser.
"Find out what you need to do, discover the quickest and best way of doing it and then write it down so everyone else does it the same way. It's all about the system. Work smart, not hard," he used to preach.
Work smart, not hard? Cycle smart, not hard? How was I going to do that when it keeps snowing, raining and hailing on me? I will have to think about it tonight and hopefully tomorrow I will have some new ideas for smart cycling – like put a motor on Valerie. Would that count as cheating? What's the definition of cycling? I'm going to buy a dictionary and look for a loophole, which somehow allows me to add an engine to Valerie without changing the 'cycling' outcome. Anything to be able to get out of the rain quicker and stop my legs from burning.

The one benefit of arriving at a campsite looking like a mermaid is that you generally get a free night because they feel sorry for you. Tonight this didn't happen. They knew I was desperate and probably charged me double. £15 was a bit steep I thought, but I wasn't going to argue. I just wanted a shower. I had a very long shower and used the hand dryer to dry my socks. Anything to use more energy in order to speed up global warming. Anything to make the cold go away.

By the time I had set up camp and all warmed up, it had cleared a bit. I noticed there was a pub about a mile back down the road so decided to treat myself. I jumped back on Valerie, who had lost a lot of weight in the last hour with all the tent unpacking etc. She was a different animal and I zoomed down the lane. I'm surely as fast as Bradley Wiggins now, I thought. All this training on a heavy bike must have done some good, although it's probably just brought forward the onset of arthritis in my knees. Ah well. By the time I'm 60, you'll be able to buy bionic legs anyway.

The pub was fairly quiet. The bar lady, or girl as she was only in her early 20's at the most, seemed pretty bored. I think it's because she was chewing gum. That always makes people look bored. She had long dark hair and I first dismissed her as just another grumpy bored bar lady.

It was only once she had poured my pint and I was sitting down in the corner that I noticed something about her. I couldn't put my finger on it. She looked like she had a story. I wanted to speak to her but was too shy. In any case there was another quite large scary man at the bar already trying for her attention. She wasn't listening to him though which meant he must be a local she knows. If not then she's just rude. Interesting, but rude. Oh well. I'll just pretend she's a Russian Spy or something.

After a few beers and trying to think of as many scenarios as to why a Russian Spy was working as a bar lady near Wales, I jumped back on Valerie and cycled back in the pitch dark to the campsite. Really should get cycle lights.

Hail built up on tent. Still cold!

A canal. Duh!

Mortimer's Cross to Whitchurch

Holy cow, it was cold last night. Seriously! Will this ever end? I'm thinking that this whole cycling in April may not have been the best idea. At least the uphill theory has been disproven. It's quite flat now. I - *ahem* - knew that all along really!

It was so cold the only useful idea I could come up with was to eat more chocolate for energy. That's hardly smart cycling, but it may help. Looking at the map there is nothing but boring flat straight roads for most of today with no major excitement along the way. I might use today to really eat up the miles so that I can have more time later on when the scenery is better.

I head out onto the back roads for an early start and as usual it starts raining. Good thing there is nothing to look at around here. I keep my head low while concentrating on the road and trying to avoid the deathly slippery white lines.

Although it's flat, it's still a slog trying to push a bike that should be on the Atkins Diet to any sort of reasonable pace. I always get excited when I reach double figures on the speedo. Getting up to speed takes about 3 years but once I'm there then it's OK. Every now and then I have to slow down for a squirrel - WHY ARE YOU ON THE ROAD YOU STUPID ANIMAL????? - and it takes forever to get over 10mph again.

The hours and miles roll on by which brings with it a new challenge. I keep repeating in my head, over and over again, each song that I hear from a passing car. This song stays with me until another car playing loud music zooms past, bringing with it a new song. I wish someone with good music taste would play their stereos loudly while driving past me, but instead it's always the rude boys with their trans-jungle-drum-and-house or whatever you call it. (I'm sounding very old right now, aren't I?) At least the fast beat keeps me alive and pedalling in time with the song. Singing along to Beethoven's 246th Symphony might make me fall asleep. I don't really like Beethoven either by the way and also have no idea how many symphonies he made.

The cold and the boring flat roads have made me shut down a little. I don't seem to remember anything. I cycled for nearly an hour and literally could not remember a single thing. In fact it may have been 3 hours. Except I'd probably me a lot more hungry if that were true. This is autopilot on a whole new level. Before I know it I've made it to Shrewsbury. I'm happy to tell you that Shrewsbury is not a Market Town . . . wait no, my bad. It is, in fact, a Market Town. Actually it even tries to one-up itself by saying it's a Medieval Market Town. I like that. It certainly has a lot going on including a castle that some king or earl or someone else important who wore long socks over their trousers lived in. Some Abbeys. Quite a few black and white wooden houses, and so on. Can you tell I didn't listen during History lessons at school? Actually, history fans, Charles Robert Darwin was born in Shrewsbury. That much I know. There! I pulled it back.

It's early afternoon by the time I've finished with Shrewsbury. I had a pie and Coke for lunch followed by a coffee and a Lion bar. It's not my favourite chocolate bar but I like the name. It makes me feel stronger, plus my ginger mane and facial hair make me look a little like a lion too.

My route takes me north out of Shrewsbury as if I'm heading toward Liverpool. I don't plan on cycling through Liverpool (nothing against Liverpool, just hate cycling through cities) so will take a big detour east of Manchester tomorrow. But for now, I don't need to worry and can just put my head down. I forgot to mention but it started to rain as I was leaving Shrewsbury. It's almost not worth writing about. In fact, if I don't mention it, consider it wet.

The road north was pretty much the same as earlier. Very flat and not much to see. I shut down again with my head low and shoulders hunched over. It was depressing to know that I still have 2 or 3 more days of this. Once I'm past Manchester, then things will get better. That thought alone is keeping my legs turning.

By 4 pm it is way too cold and wet to carry on, and I decide to camp up in a small campsite down a bumpy green lane. I'm just outside Whitchurch. It's very clean (the campsite, not the town – the town might be clean but I haven't seen it yet) and as always, empty. I even put my entire tent up in autopilot mode.

Today has been flat, cold and wet. Besides a few cool looking piles of bricks that make a building in Shrewsbury, it has been pretty mind numbing. I wonder if it is better when the sun is shining? Maybe if I hadn't spent the entire day with my head in my lap, I'd have noticed a few more things.

Alas, it's not summer, it's winter and I just have to get on with it.

Dinner is packet pasta and the evening is spent looking at my route for tomorrow. I did some good miles today which means I'm almost certain to make it past Manchester the day after tomorrow. I have always wanted to go through the Peak District. I hear it's quite beautiful out there even if the word 'Peak' sends cramp down my legs.

Although my fitness is getting much better I still battle up hills because of all the weight Valerie is carrying. I am now heading northeast towards Manchester which should give me good enough time to get past it the day after tomorrow. I am a little nervous, as I really don't want to get stuck in the centre of a town like I did in Exeter. Anything to avoid hostels and cities. Have I said that enough?

I mentioned briefly my big beard earlier but it's, I think, a personal best. It's not often one gets to see a huge ginger beard. The last time I grew a beard was in Tibet. Tibetans, not being ones for much facial hair, found my beard somewhat of a tourist attraction. I, of course, being the tourist, and the attraction at the same time. People would walk up to me with huge smiles while touching their faces and blowing up their cheeks to impersonate my beard.

At one point, one guy came and shook my hand. He was very friendly. The guy behind him saw this and also wanted to shake my hand. I did so obligingly thinking he too was very friendly. After smiling and nodding (as this is all I could do in Tibet for their complete lack of English and my complete lack of Chinese/Mandarin) I looked up to see a queue of about 8 Tibetans all wanting to shake my hand. I think I managed 5 of them before I saw many more wanting to get involved. I had to just laugh and stand back with my hands in the air. Everyone laughed as I think they all saw my dilemma. Good times.

I don't think I am quite going to get the same reaction here but having a huge beard always brings back fun memories. I guess this trip will be added to the memory bank of stories with the common theme of 'Huge Beard'. It's almost like how smells remind you of certain things. Whenever I grow a beard again, it'll remind me of this trip.

Route planned and belly full, I wrap up warm and fall asleep. Empty campsites might be slightly boring but at least they are very quiet.

At least it's flat in this part of the world

Another empty campsite

Whitchurch to Macclesfield

It's 7.30 am. I've been sleeping well lately. Although cold, I managed to keep snug and still really impressed with my new tent. I have 2 more days of pretty boring cycling as I try and work my way around Liverpool and Manchester. To avoid landing up lost on a council estate in Manchester at midnight, I'm going to make the most of my aunt and uncle, Trish and Gavin, who live in Macclesfield, which is just southeast of the city, where I don't want to land up. Have I mentioned that I don't like cities? I'll stop now! Little Flying Cow seems to be laughing at me in the hope I do get lost.

It's quite cold so I decide to stay on 'A' roads. The going is fast and I am making good time. It's definitely getting busier and busier the closer I get to Manchester.

Everything was going well until I went the wrong way down a very busy dual carriageway. Not the wrong way as in cycling into oncoming traffic, but rather I went east instead of north. The problem was I couldn't just turn around because of the central barrier. I looked at my map and realised the next exit was at least 5 miles away. That would add an hour to my ride. I had no other choice but to turn around here and somehow try get over the central barrier. I seemed to wait a lifetime for a gap in traffic but eventually made a dash for it. I pushed Valerie off the road onto the gravel bit in the middle and she practically sank a foot down.

I struggled onto the barrier and tried to pick her up. It was no use. Valerie was way too heavy for me to lift over. I'd have to take off all my panniers. To make things worse, it started to rain again.

"Come on!!!! Can I get a break here?"

It's not often that I get angry but I was pretty close to a severe sense of humour failure as I stood there, drenched to the bone, in the middle of a busy dual carriageway trying to take off and put back very heavy panniers while my annoying mascot was playing the smallest violin in the world, just for me.

"Damn you rain, bugger off."

I didn't care I was shouting out loud. I just wanted to get dry and make it past Manchester and dual carriageways, and cars, and fumes, and, and, and, argh!!!!!

After messing around for ages trying to get my panniers back on with numb fingers, I was heading back to the roundabout where I originally got lost. I didn't make the same mistake twice and once back on the right road, put my head down to make up for lost time.

All I could think of was Gavin's roasts which are the best in the world. No time for sight seeing. No time to take in the scenery. I just wanted to get there and eat. I apologise if you live southwest of Macclesfield. I am sure it is in fact very pretty but today wasn't the day I was going to find out. I'll come back another day – when it's sunny!

By 3 pm I reach Macclesfield and get lost again so give Gavin a call to get better directions. I tell them where I am, (at a pub of course,) and it's not long before he arrives in his car.

"Hey Seano, You've made it. Well done hey." Gavin shouts out the window as he drives into the car park.

"Thanks Gav, pretty tired though."

"I bet you're hungry, follow me. Not far now."

I follow Gav through some scenic back streets to their home. Gavin and Trish haven't changed a bit. They look exactly the same as I remember them from when I was 5 years old. I have only seen them once since they moved from Zimbabwe. Gavin is my father's brother and was another victim of Uncle Bob's (what Zimbabweans call Robert Mugabe) destructive regime. They gave up everything in 2001 and moved over here. They now live in Manchester where it rains all year. Fair play to them as they have made the best of a pretty awful situation and have never looked back. Right. That's enough of a mood killer. Let's move on!

All I can think of is roast and I wasn't disappointed. As I enter the kitchen, I can smell one of Gavin's signature roasts. Yes please. Chicken! My mouth starts watering. I'm practically drooling on the carpet, which is not a good look by the way. Unfortunately for me, Gavin and Trish have a habit of eating quite late so I am forced to wait in agony. We sit down and chat about Africa, old times and as always what a knob Uncle Bob is. I hate getting to indepth into Zimbabwe politics. Everyone knows it's a joke that nothing has been done but as long as Bob is friends with the Chinese, or someone finds oil, then that's just the way it's going to stay. You can get all depressed by it but you'll probably die depressed, so it's best to move forward. Gavin and Trish have done that and I admire their resilience. Having to leave everything and everyone you know and love because of some insane twat must be hard. (I called Mugabe a twat. If I mysteriously disappear in the next few weeks it's because he has read this and sent one of his minions to *'take care of me'*.)

Dinner is soon ready and I pile in. Must get food in me. Conversation dies down for a bit as I stuff my face with the juiciest potatoes I've ever had. I barely look up and when I am done I realise Gavin and Trish have hardly dented their meal. Oh God! I've become a human vacuum cleaner. Now that's a good look. I'm going to be single for the rest of my life, which means I won't get to climb Kilimanjaro with my future 16 year old child. That doesn't stop me from having seconds and thirds though. Food is more important than sleep, or conversation, or even table manners for that matter.

Trish has the greenest fingers off all time. Her garden is amazing considering it's cold and raining most of the year. Actually all year. Their home in Zimbabwe was practically a botanical garden complete with Koi ponds and everything. It's embarrassing talking to her about plants. I killed a cactus once which I'm not even sure is actually possible, but I managed it. Maybe I shouldn't have children!

By 9 pm I'm ready for bed, an actual bed at that, and make my way up to, um, bed. Bed, bed, bed. The second most exciting word in the world, after roast. Horrible day on the road made better by catching up with family, eating a chicken, calling Mugabe a twat, and reliving old times!

Talking to a horse – too much time alone

Oh look. It's about to rain again

Macclesfield to Settle

I am awoken by bright rays coming through the window. Did you hear that? SUN!!!! No way? It can't be actual sunshine? Yes!

My bleary eyes struggle to see the time but through the haze I see that it's 6.30 am. It's a little earlier than I normally wake up, but I feel fresh and happy that it is sunny. I get up slowly and make my way downstairs for some cereal and toast. It's nice to know that I don't have to pack up my tent. Gavin and Trish hear that I am awake and come down to see me off.

I feel bad that I've woken them up but they don't mind and Trish has sorted me a sandwich for the road. She is great like that. I pack up everything, have another coffee and hit the road. As I am just about to leave, Trish gives me £20 towards the charity. Such a lovely gesture. I wave goodbye and start hurtling down the road before realising I've gone the wrong way so have that awkward moment of turning around and cycling past them again.

No sooner had I gotten onto the main road, it started to rain again. And not your average rain either. It was bucketing it down, drowned rat style. My feet and fingers soon lose all their feeling and I am forced to stop for another breakfast and coffee. My addiction for coffee is getting stronger and stronger but I don't care. I am not sure if I love the coffee or love the idea of stopping in a small town in a quaint coffee shop. Either way, I love it.

Turns out I totally overcompensated on the whole 'go well east of Manchester' idea, because the roads were not nearly as bad as I thought they'd be. Result! This part of the trip was pretty uneventful and certainly didn't satisfy my adventurous side. Long flat roads that were quite urban with loads of traffic lights. I soon settle into the routine of cycle, stop, cycle, stop, cycle, stop and so on. You get the idea!

I was just falling into deep thought when a car raced passed me and braked quickly. The driver then jumped out the car. Oh no! I'm just about to get mugged. Good luck to them trying to get my panniers off, and picking Valerie up was not going to happen either. I was more worried about stopping in time. I damn nearly crashed into them – Valerie's stopping distance isn't as good as it used to be now that she's put all this weight on.

I couldn't pass them either because they were half on the pavement and half on the busy road. Right! If I get mugged then at least a car will see it. Just don't take my journal. I slammed on my brakes and came to a nails-on-a-blackboard screeching halt about 2 metres from the car.

A man jumped out and started walking towards me. He was smiling and holding something in his hand. Great, he is one of those muggers who leads you into a false sense of security before stabbing you in the back?

"Mate, just read the back of your jersey. That's great what you are doing it is. I just thought I'd stop and give you a fiver."

"Wow, so you're not going to mug me then?"

"Sorry?"

115

"Um. Nothing! Thank you, that's very kind of you. You've just saved 5 hedgehogs."
(Can I just say that it's probably more than £1 to save a hedgehog so please don't send the C.P.R.E. just £1 and expect one of those hedgehog toys and a monthly hedgehog newsletter.)

We chatted briefly and then they sped off again. I, on the other hand, took about 5 hours to get back up to speed. This always happens when I stop. My legs get cold and decide they've had enough. Little Flying Cow loves seeing me in pain. Bastard!

At around 3 pm with far too many stops to warm my hands under my armpits, I decide to take some 'B' roads. I spent most of the next two hours in granny gear, sweating like a convict on death row but at least I was warm, and finally the scenery got better, a lot better.

I've spent the last few days cycling through pretty flat, dull, busy industrial Britain, so to finally have a small brick wall within spitting distance on both sides of me (I actually tried this) makes me extremely happy.

A warm sense of peace and calm starts to completely relaxes me. My head isn't hanging low anymore and I've forgotten what my groin looks like. Never thought I'd say that. It's really hilly but I don't care at all. I'll never complain about hills again if the scenery is this good. It's far better than flat and boring! With each stone cottage and grazing sheep, I can feel the stress from the last few days leaving me. It helps that it is slightly sunnier than normal which always helps in lifting my spirits off the sodden tarmac.

There is only one main campsite on the map and it's

near Settle. That works out perfectly. I'm not quite going into Settle so decide to stop for some gourmet dinner supplies - packet pasta and a beer. Gordon Ramsey beware! It's far off my roast from last night but it'll do. If you have roast every day then it loses its appeal right? Yes. That's what I'm going with anyway.

I'm no more than 5 miles from the campsite and I am already thinking about a warm shower. Once you've tasted one warm shower, it's hard to go back to wet wipes and cold basins. My pace slows as it always does towards the end of the day and it's 5 pm by the time I reach the campsite. I found the reception and walked in practically backwards. I did this in the hope the middle-aged man behind the counter would read it and give me a free night's stay. I had a 50/50 success rate which I thought to be quite good.

"Good evening Sir, I see you've been doing some cycling," he said with a slight sorry look on his face.

"Just a bit," I laughed

"You're going to hate me when I tell you we don't accept tents here. We're a caravan campsite only."

Noooo!!!!! This can't be? The next campsite is miles away and my brain is pretty much in a hot shower already. Graham, as I read on his nametag, must have sensed my distressed look and followed up with.

"But seeing as it's late and cold, I'm sure we can make a plan."

Ah, what beautiful words. Graham is my new favourite person.

"Follow me mate. I'll put you somewhere where the owner won't find you."

Graham took me round the back of a series of permanent

caravans which looked very sketchy and if he hadn't told me about the fact we were trying to hide I'd have been a little worried.

"There we go mate. That should do you fine. Here is the code for the shower room. Go get yourself showered. You look like you need it."

Normally I'd have been offended by someone telling me I need to have a shower but I really did. Although it was cold, I did sweat a lot on the hills during the final two hours. Also I really should have washed my clothes at Gavin and Trish's. Rookie! I'll work out this cycle touring thing eventually!

"How much do I owe you, mate?" I asked.

"No bother man. We don't have a section on the system for tents so there is no point."

So from nearly not having a place to camp, I now had a camp spot, a warm shower and didn't have to pay for it. Happy Sean. A long day but glad to be out the hustle and bustle of middle England. Bring on the lakes.

More scenic back roads

Great to be heading towards the lakes

Settle to Windermere

Good morning 7 am. It is still so cold and getting out of my sleeping bag takes on a whole new level of courage, which I don't have, so I decide to lie in and wait for the sun to warm things up. I'm getting quite good at eating my cereal while lying down. (Much harder than it sounds – go on, try it!)

By 8 am it's still cold and there is no point in waiting any longer. I'd be here for another 3 weeks if I were going to wait for things to get warmer. With that, and a coffee inside me, I vibrated out of bed and started packing up. I can barely put my tent back in the bag and my fingers freeze to the poles each time I touch them. Eventually I give up and run a basin of warm water and submerge my hands into the tingling water. They look blue and distorted. I look like Gollum. I stand there for at least 10 minutes pretending I'm trying to find The Ring in a crocodile infested pond before I dare carry on packing up.

It starts to rain as I get back on the road. I'm not even annoyed by it anymore. (I am secretly but trying to be positive.) Rain is now just an inevitable way of life for me and I have to just deal with it. Maybe I'll grow gills and be able to breath underwater, finally. It is debatable whether I am in fact actually 'dealing' with it though. Reading back on my journal suggests borderline madness. Plus didn't I just spend 10 minutes looking for a fictional ring in a made up pond? Oh dear!

My route today is to head westwards towards the Lakes. I can't actually wait. I have never been to the Lake District before and it's one of the reasons I am on Valerie for a month instead of CHAV'ing it up in Spain. To see Britain - as much of it as possible. From Settle I stay on the main road to get some fast miles in. The quicker I get to the Lakes, the more time I can spend there.

By 11 am the rain had eased but there was still that ever-present threatening sky all around. Coincidentally, much like scenes from Lord of the Rings. Maybe the Gollum thing wasn't a dream. Every now and then the sun finds a gap in the clouds. In that moment the entire landscape bursts into a colourful array of early spring greens and browns. It's all a bit short-lived as the sun disappears behind the next flock of clouds and the landscape seems to let out a huge sigh as if rolling over and going back to sleep. The hills are getting steeper and steeper but my good mood overrides any pain in my legs.

I reach the coastal town of Milnthorpe by lunchtime and because I am on the coast I am in the mood for fish and chips. I'm full of clichés I am! Turns out I had no other choice anyway because all I could find were fish and chip shops. I stop outside the one that has the best place to chain Valerie up and go inside.

It's very empty. I am not sure if the restaurant part is open but the owner is very excited to have me. He even brings his laptop out and finds out about my trip online. The fish and chips were the best I've ever had and again I didn't have to pay. When I returned to Valerie, I was pleasantly surprised to find 69p on her seat. Yet again a little gesture lifts my mood even further.

"That's awesome, Little Flying Cow. Look someone left some money for us," I said while laughing to myself.

"So how many hedgehogs does 69p save?"

"I am not sure but I think at least half a hedgehog."

The idea of trying to save half a hedgehog was completely ridiculous yet I still tried to think of ways to save half a hedgehog without having to kill it. The mind boggles.

"Don't be dumbass," said Little Flying Cow. "You don't use the 69p now! You save it until you have enough to save a whole hedgehog and then use it."

Of course I knew the answer, but it still didn't stop my mind from wandering all over the place. That has been happening a lot these last few days. Too much time alone.

I am a little ahead of schedule today so decide to cut through some 'B' roads to join up with the southerly tip of Windermere so that I can cycle along it until I find a campsite.

20 minutes later . . .

Oh my helmet, are the hills steep. Windermere can't be more than a few hundred feet above sea level but it feels like I'm in the Alps. The slippery winding roads through the forest are beautiful though. At least I think they are because I am spending half the time with my chest on the handlebars staring down at my front mudguard. I am leaning so far forward that every now and then I press my horn with my chest, and as this always makes me laugh I inevitably lose momentum.

Most of the weight on Valerie is in the back two

panniers and I very nearly do a wheelie every time I lean back in the saddle. I even start to wheel spin on the slippery moss covered shaded corners. I must be working at a 108% heart rate and pretty much have to catch my heart in my hand and push it back with every beat. I lose all my other senses too and at the top of the 625th (4th) hill, I turn around to see a queue of cars behind me.

I hope I haven't been keeping them too long? I am sure they feel sorry for me, so I move over and just smile and wave them by. The first two cars clearly feel sorry for me and are pretty smiley but the others are grumpy because I guess they couldn't see what the holdup was. They just roar passed in the aggressive way people do when trying to enforce their presence on the road when annoyed. Come on. We all do it.

Eventually, after I've cleared my lungs from exhaust fumes, I make the summit (yes it was a proper *summit* and don't care what you say – in fact, isn't Scafell Pike somewhere around here? I must have cycled up it by mistake) and am greeted with the most breath-taking views so far. And taking a breath is exactly what I needed so I pulled over into a lay-by to soak it all in. I'm pretty sure I left my right lung on that last hill, but didn't care anymore. That was so 5 minutes ago. I was in a new world now.

Windermere lay below the never-ending sprawl of mountains going into the distance. Some trees had started to turn green while others were still bare. I could practically see Spring happening in front of me. All thoughts of sore legs and bouncing heart were a long distant memory.

Two days ago, I was stressed about getting stuck in

the middle of overpopulated industrial Britain and now I couldn't see or hear anything except a few birds, a billion trees and a dark skyline. How was I in the same country? Maybe I wasn't? This did look a lot like Canada. Mmmmm?

I could have stayed and enjoyed that view for a lifetime but it was still chilly so decided to head down towards the lake and find a spot for the night. It wasn't long before I found a campsite. It was still early season but being the Lakes meant there were quite a few people camped up already. I got the standard glares as I wandered through the site looking for a good spot. The lack of washing, my slightly dodgy beard and drunk-like fatigue gave me the perfect homeless person look. I was half tempted to put one of my water bottles in a brown paper bag. That would turn a few heads but probably not a good idea for the charity side of things.

I prefer to be away from everyone when I camp. I use the excuse that I have bat-like ears and if someone is snoring in the tent next to me then I'll never sleep, but in reality, I smell – a lot!

All set up, and showered I must add, I decided to treat myself to a proper pub meal (not packet pasta) and much deserved beer. The campsite had its own restaurant and bar. I walked in and blimey it was packed. I walked to the bar and no-one even looked at me. That's strange, I thought but then realised I wasn't in my cycle gear. I could hear Little Flying Cow shouting from back at the tent:

"It's not always about you, you vain idiot."

Twerp. I knew that but when you've spent the past two weeks with people nearly running you over to find out what you are doing, you kind of get into the zone of it all. Anyway, it was nice to sit down, have a well-earned beer and update my journal. I bought a vintage one. Journal that is, not beer. One that you need a string to close. I felt like an early century explorer whenever I opened it to make a note. The only thing missing was the feather pen. Someone needs to design a modern one of those. I'd buy it! There must be one. I'll write a note in my vintage notebook to look that up. Done!

In my excitement to write my journal, I managed to knock over my precious beer. Mmmyyyy precccciousss!! (Sorry! I just had to add that.) It went everywhere. Now the entire pub was looking at me along with the obligatory "Wheeeey!" from a rowdy bunch in the corner. Don't you just love that? I mopped it up awkwardly and got another one. About five minutes later, a gentleman came over. He was part of the rowdy bunch. He probably wants to knock over my second pint too.

"Hello mate, have you ruined your Uni notes?"

"Um, sorry?"

"I saw you spilled your pint and was wondering if your Uni notes got wet?"

What a nice guy. He was coming over just to see if I had messed up some notes for University. I'm glad he still thinks I go to University – thank you Nivea for Men! I explained what I was doing. By now I could get all the key points down in one sentence. Cycle, Britain, Charity, Camping, Solo, Unsupported, Rain! That's basically it, with some creativity and hardship thrown in to add some jeopardy.

"That's amazing, good on ya. Hold right there."

And before I could even say anything, he was off. The pub was kind of 'L' shaped and he disappeared around the corner. After about a minute, I stopped looking where he was and carried on writing my journal. I wasn't going anywhere. Five minutes later he came back and put £80 on the table.

"I am so impressed with what you are doing, I just did a whip-round the pub and we wanted to give this to you for your charity."

I was speechless. Just when I thought I'd seen all the generosity I could, I get blown away again. This adventure is truly reinstalling my faith in humanity. Stress City seemed a far distant planet from where I was now. Could I ever go back? Well, yes of course I could, but I didn't want too.

After much appreciation and the 2nd best lasagne I have had on this trip, I headed back to my tent. Talked some nonsense with Little Flying Cow and hit the sack. What a great day. Tomorrow I'd be going into the real Lake District. I couldn't wait.

Frost covered pannier

First view of the lakes

Windermere to Carlisle(ish)

Best sleep ever and guess what - it isn't raining. I keep mentioning the rain and I can usually take whatever is thrown at me but it's just SO MUCH BETTER when it's dry. The day got better as I freewheeled all the way down to the lakeshore. There is nothing better than getting 5 miles under the belt without even turning your legs. It certainly lifts the spirits.

The more I cycled along the shore, the more convinced I became that I had somehow landed up in Canada. The early morning mist hovered just inches above the mirror like water. Geese and ducks floated along the banks looking for breakfast. I can't remember a time when I felt this much calm. It was in fact so calm that it was a little overwhelming. Now that's an oxymoron if I've ever heard of one. It was true though. Quite hard to explain.

Finding a lakeshore café for breakfast was the next goal, which wasn't hard at all. I found a quaint one situated on the waterfront. It had a red telephone box outside it, which was blatantly bought by the owner and didn't work at all. The café was surprisingly busy for this time of the morning. Maybe it's the weekend? I found a free table and settled in for, you guessed it, a 3-2-1 and a huge coffee. I noticed two American girls sitting next to me. Actually, maybe they were Canadian. It's all making sense now! I decided to make conversation to check.

"So, do you come here often?"

Oh God, did that sound like a chat-up line. Idiot. I was trying to be ironic because they were from America/Canada and this was England (hopefully) and . . . and . . . I'm giving up. It is funny how you get disconnected from who you are in 'real life' when you are in cycle gear and on a crazy adventure. It's like wearing fancy dress. For a moment you are someone else.

As you've worked out by now I'm quite shy when it comes to approaching girls but now I'm Sean Conway - The Adventurer. It sounded a lot better in my head but nevertheless it gave me the confidence to chat to some good looking girls with the cool type of American/Canadian accents. Is there really a difference?

"Haha, no we are just like here on holiday. Does it like always rain so much?"

"I'm afraid so."

I hadn't noticed, but it had started raining again. Rats!

"So I take it you're like doing some cycling?" one of them said in a giddy way. They were quite excitable and clearly still in the whole 'Wow, England is so pretty and look at the cute red phone boxes' phase.

"Yeah, I'm cycling the length of this small island for charity. I think I'm halfway."

By now I'm trying to put on my best Hugh Grant accent, and failing dismally. They are buying it though.

"Wow, that's like so amazing. How long has it like taken you?"

These two said 'like' nearly as much as the moustached fellow from a week ago. They made it sound cool though.

"Two weeks so far and another two weeks to go. I'm kind of over the rain though. It's rubbish."

"Hehe, rubbish? Is that like saying it's trash? That's so

cute."
Wow, it's too easy to make these girls laugh. Americanism banter – I'm all over it! My newfound confidence giving me a big head. Little Flying Cow was influencing me again. We chatted for a little longer but there is only so long you can stay in a café after you've finished everything and the waitress has cleared your table. We said goodbyes and I hit the road again. I felt very happy. I had had a good breakfast, talked to actual girls, and wasn't in Canada.

The route along Windermere continued to amaze me. Why have I never been to the Lakes before? I kept saying to myself to which Little Flying Cow would always reply.
"Because you've sold out to Stress City. You're a Pink Tie without a pink tie."
He had a point. How did an African born bush boy land up in one of the busiest cities in the world?

Here in the Lakes I see people in their little stone cottages high up in the woods with smoke bellowing out their chimneys. They have a small, but adequate, flock of sheep grazing in the field below. This makes me wish for a simpler life.

I want to live in one of those cottages one day. Growing up in Post Colonial Africa meant that throughout school we were fed the romantic picture postcard idea of Britain, fuelled by books like Wind in the Willows and the Secret Garden. I spent many an afternoon in my own secret garden, painting a picture (metaphorically - I can't paint) of ivy-covered stone walls, robins in holly bushes, rabbits frolicking on emerald green fields and small lakes surrounded by huge willow trees with a disused upturned wooden rowing boat now used by a badger as his home. I think there might have even been a red phone box somewhere too. Basically think of every British countryside cliché and put it in one scene. That's what I imagined.

All of these romantic visuals were far off the African reality of 35-degree heat and sand blasted scrubland, where you risk death from various creatures at least 7 times a day. It may have been adventurous, but not romantic. So to finally be in a part of the world that was a carbon copy of my wild childhood imagination was a little mind-boggling.

A few times I couldn't work out whether I had actually seen some rabbits playing in a field or was just remembering a scene from a childhood memory. I can't remember a time when my mind was this imaginative. That's the one thing I hate about getting older. Imagination takes a back seat for the sometimes harsh reality of real life. Wow. That was deep. Where's that orange rabbit I just saw?

I carried on through the Lakes deep in thought and before I knew it I was half way out the other side. What? It's so small. I couldn't believe it. All I wanted to do was stay there, build a fire and do some fishing with a Davy Crocket hat on.

I researched my map and found a smaller road that went along the quieter west side of one of the smaller lakes north of Windermere. This would add a few miles to my ride through the Lakes. I had gone past the road already so backtracked about half a mile. Normally I get really annoyed with going back on myself but anything to add more time in the Lakes was a good thing.

The west side road was even more beautiful and a lot quieter. There were a few times when the entire road was blocked by a million pink sheep. I've always wondered if there is any logic behind the colour people paint their sheep. Was pink the last colour left? I'd paint mine with black spots to make them look like Dalmatians, just to confuse my sheep dog.

I was glad I was on this side road because I could see the traffic building up on the east shore. Huge tour busses bombing along bringing with them more excitable American girls. Wait! Actually! Maybe I need to be back on that road!

I slowed my pace right down so that I could spend more time in the Lakes. For the first time, I wasn't actually annoyed that I was going slower than 10mph. My little detour soon ended and I was back on the main road. The going was slow as I climbed and climbed, slowly up to Kirkstone Pass. This was the final climb before descending to Keswick and out of the Lakes. This made me sad.

By the time I was out of the Lakes and back on to busy roads, I was firmly back to the harsh reality of rain. It was pissing it down and I was pretty much cycling in a river and couldn't feel my hands and feet anymore. They had probably been numb for ages. It's funny how strong the mind is. I was so deep in thought that I hadn't realised. Is that what meditation is? I might try it when I get home.

I really needed to stop. It became too dangerous to cycle because my reaction time was practically non-existent, and my head bowed so far down all I was looking at was my groin again. Not the best view I've had. (No ginger related jokes please.) I found another empty campsite and after an hour trying to find the manager so I could get into the shower room, found out there was no hot water. BUT! And this is a big one. They had a tumble dryer! Oh yes! Dry clothes at last. It was 3 pm, the earliest I had stopped since I began but just couldn't carry on. I was too cold. Luckily I had one spare packet pasta left so was able to eat some dinner. I boiled it up and spent a few hours reading 'The Power of One' by Bryce Courtenay. The book was based in the part of Africa where I grew up, which made me a little homesick at times. Especially now that I'm feeling all sorry for myself. It still remains my favourite book of all time. I also tried to write a few pages in my journal but it was completely soaked through. I'd have to dry the pages out first before I could write on them.

I also needed to make a plan about my feet. They were just getting too wet from the spray coming off the road when I cycled through a puddle. I spent a good half an hour studying the design of a toe strap touring pedal and eventually came up with a high-tech contraption to divert water from hitting my foot – a Tesco bag! Yes. That's right. I just wrapped a plastic bag around the toe strap, which made a little cove for my foot to go inside. This would then stop any water hitting my foot. Dragons Den here I come.

By dark I was ready for sleep. A pretty early night but I could feel myself getting hungry and figured if I am at least asleep then I'll not feel the effects. With that I nodded off, fantasizing about my future life in a stone cottage.

Beautiful Lake Windermere

Tesco packet pedal cover

Carlisle(ish) to Moffat

I'm practically dying of hunger. Last night's 250 kcal packet pasta meal vaporised before it even hit my stomach. Must get an early breakfast - fast. Turns out it's a Sunday and nothing is open. Seriously?

I really need to sort my nutrition strategy out. You'd have thought I would have learned by now. I could feel my legs being eaten away as my body started to burn muscle tissue as an energy source. Of course that wasn't happening but in my mind I was becoming a skeleton.

Little Flying Cow hits me with a joke. "So a skeleton walks into a bar and asks the barmen: Can I have a pint . . . and a mop."

Crap joke. I really need some food.

The road heading out of the Lakes was quite busy. All the huge mountains in The Lakes, or around them, means there is only one proper main road heading towards Carlisle and I, along with many trucks was on it. At least it was still downhill and Sunday so wasn't that busy. The beautiful mountains of the Lakes gave way to a more open flatland the further north I went.

I saw a bunch of club cyclist all getting ready for their Sunday morning ride. I felt jealous that they were going cycling with a bike that weighed less than one of my panniers. I naturally stepped up my game a bit as I went

135

past, trying my best not to look like death. I think I pulled that one off as we gave each other a quick ride-by howdy. I am finally starting to feel like I know what I am doing on a bike.

Just then the peloton zoomed past me as if I was in reverse and I was put firmly back in my place. Who was I kidding? It's taken me two weeks to do 728 miles. I have no idea what to do if I break a spoke, a chain or my wheel becomes untrue. I'm not even sure I know what untrue means. I'm not really even sure I know how to fix a puncture properly either. Luckily I haven't had to yet. Thank you really-heavy-puncture-proof tyres that came with Valerie. Not even sure what you are but thank you!

From the Lakes it's a long gentle downhill to Carlisle. I'm not sure what I would have done if it were all uphill. I had no energy and really needed some food. I'm sure the scenery was pretty but the little energy I had was used to stay on the road.

By the time I reached Carlisle it was still too early for any 3-2-1 serving café to be open. Why does it have to be Sunday? Come on! There must be somewhere to find food. Then I saw it, towering over the treetops. No! Really? Surely there is a better option? Not The Golden Arches? I don't really do fast food. Not because I am one of those people who boycott places like McDonalds, but rather because I think if I wanted to eat cardboard I wouldn't spend £5.75 doing so. They do make good coffee though and by now my love affair with that dark roasted bean is quite out of control. I have no option. Nothing else is open.

The next 20 minutes aren't suitable for printing. It got

messy!

After pigging out on some overpriced cardboard with ketchup and a coffee the size of China, I leave Carlisle and plan to use the old Glasgow road, which follows the highway. The Highway Agency however have other plans for me and I am forced onto some small back roads because of roadworks. I didn't mind though. They were quiet and it wasn't raining. No rain – No complain! Yeah! That's my C+ for poem writing at junior school shining through right there!

The going was fast and flat. I loved seeing all the small towns and farmhouses. Being chased by a few dogs was the order of the day but none of them were scary. No matter how hard they bark, the Dulux dog will always look cute and cuddly.

The one problem with cycling the back roads is finding food. Wasn't it just yesterday that I said I must sort out my nutrition? When will I learn? Never, is the correct answer.

At around lunchtime, I passed through a small area where every house was painted the same colour. White walls with turquoise-blue window and door frames. I started to wonder how that came about? Was there a local meeting where they all decided to do the same? If so, was turquoise-blue the first choice of colour or did someone have 764 litres sitting in their garage. I'd have chosen orange myself (It's a ginger thing) but pretty sure I'd have been alone on that vote.

"I would totally paint mine orange if I bought a house here. Just to annoy people," said Little Flying Cow.

Typical! Always looking to stir things up.

By 4.30 pm, loads of back roads and a long downhill I was in Moffat. I was starving. I think I saw more dogs than people today. I found a very busy campsite, had the best shower in the world, (that happens every time I have a hot shower nowadays) and went into town for a 16oz steak and chips. Bring on the protein. Fix me!

I realised that I also might be in Scotland. I wasn't sure and didn't want to walk up to someone looking like a complete idiot saying. "Excuse me, what country am I in?" Although Little Flying Cow wanted me to run down the street with a blue face shouting 'FREEEEDDDOOOOMMM!'

Blue face? I've got it. Maybe the turquoise-blue house people all knew someone who worked on the Braveheart filmset and that's how they got the paint. Nailed it!

I finished my meal and although felt really overfull was happy to be camping with a clear sky. At that moment I looked up and above me was an array of stars only comparable to when I was 4500m above sea level on the Tibetan Plateau. I could make out the Milky Way and one or two other constellations. OK! That's a lie, only one - Orion's Belt. Everyone knows Orion's Belt. In fact I don't think I have ever met anyone who knows any other constellations.

The moon hadn't risen yet, which made even the smallest of stars stand out. There is something magical about looking up there and wondering who is looking back? I'd spent just over two weeks alone and this made me want, even more, for there to be something out there. There must be?

I'm pretty open-minded to most things but surely you'd be daft to think we were the only ones in our solar system. With that thought, I wrapped up nicely and settled into my tent. If this was Scotland then it's good be here.

Happy that it stopped raining for a minute

Getting quite flat after the lakes

Moffat to Lanark

I wake up at 6 am and I get the best news in the world. The sun is going to be visible from the ground today. Thank goodness because I am so over the rain now. Also, and just as exciting, I get another bed tonight. I am going to stay with a very, very old friend of mine from Africa days. Old as in how long we've known each other. He's my age. I have known Craig since I was 9 years old. We went to the same junior and high school. I photographed his wedding and his brother Neil was the first, and only person to date, who has ever hit me. We were 10 and I was being annoying, as usual, so he smacked me in the face. I deserved it and we laugh about it now. (Secretly orchestrating my 23 year revenge plan.)

Craig looks a lot little like me too. Some people think we are brothers. I love this man and can't wait to see him. It's weird how you seem to see less of the people you feel the closest too. It's like your friendship is so set in stone, you know you don't have to make an effort because you will be friends forever. I still feel bad that we only get to see each other every few years. I feel even worse now that I know I can actually cycle to his house.

He lives just south of Glasgow, which *is* in Scotland. That much I know. This will be the second time I have ever been to this beautiful Highland country. The first time was donkeys years ago to photograph the Edinburgh Marathon.

It was a fly-in fly-out type job so didn't get to see much of it. So technically this is my first time. Yes. I am claiming back my Scottish virginity. You can do that. It's well documented.

Although a bit nippy at least it's sunny and after another warm shower I decide to B-line it to Craig's on the old Glasgow road. I think it's only 40 miles or so which means I'll get there early. If yesterday was Sunday, that means today is Monday (funny that) and I'll be able to get breakfast in early. That too excites me. What an exciting day ahead.

The brisk morning air flows past my head and down my back, it's just cold enough to 'wake me up', but not too cold. There is low lying mist covering the tan coloured grasslands and every now and then I hear the twit and twatter from various birds stretching their wings for their first flight of the day.

"I wonder if birds do exercise in the mornings like humans do. Look at that bunch, they are all flying together. It looks like British, um, I mean Scottish Military Fitness for birds."

Little Flying Cow was on a roll. His mind really goes off on one now and then.

"Or should I say Scottish Air Force Fitness. You know. Because they are birds."

Seriously, who thinks of this stuff? He must be going mad. He needs a coffee.

Just when Little Flying Cow and I were getting head deep into some crazy parallel bird and cow world scenario I heard a voice from behind me.

"Hello Pal."

I turned around and saw another cyclist. A middle aged

142

chap with a red bike. I couldn't pronounce the brand. It looked Italian. He seemed pretty fit and eased up next to me as I huffed and puffed up a pretty embarrassingly gentle slope. It's great to see another solo cyclist. I haven't seen many at all. Probably because most of them have better sense than to cycle around Britain in winter.

"Oh hello mate. How's it going?"

"Nee bad man, just goin' out for me morning ride like. I see you doing a bit of touring?"

He was proper Scottish with a proper Scottish accent. I do love a Scottish accent. Actually, pretty sure everyone loves a Scottish accent.

"Yes I am. I started in Land's End nearly 3 weeks ago and have been working my way up. Great to finally be in Scotland though. I love it here."

Always good to get the compliments in early. I read that in Dale Carnegie's – How to win friends and influence people.

"Bloody cold mind. At least the rain has stayed away like. You wouldn't want to be here in the wet season – which is *all year*," he laughed at his own joke.

"I think I've had my fair share of rain in England thank you very much. The closer I get to Scotland the dryer it has become."

Slight pause in the conversation as he drops back behind me to let a truck go by.

"So do you cycle a lot?" I asked.

"Yes pal, I love it like, but just been made redundant and all that shite so do an early morning ride to clear my head like."

"I'm sorry to hear that." I always feel awkward in these situations. I never know what to say. I'm really bad at condolences.

"It's OK pal, it was a shite job anyway."
We started up a hill and the conversation died for a bit as we both panted our way up into the morning light. OK. It was only me panting.
"Right pal, you have a good day. Must get back to the wife like."
And with that he turned around and was off. I didn't even know his name.

The old Glasgow road literally follows the motorway all the way up towards, you guessed it, Glasgow. I don't know why they just didn't get rid of it. I'm not complaining though. It's really quiet and has a good hard shoulder. I can't imagine that this was at one point the only way to get to Glasgow from the south. It must have taken forever.

By 9 am it started to close in again and by 9.30 am it actually started to snow. Yes, you heard it right. Snow! What happened to all that sunshine all day malarky? To top it off, a killer headwind decided to blow from the north. Remember the hamster/syrup/wind situation. Now throw it in a fridge. That's what it was like.
"Haha, you're a goner mate." Little Flying Cow was at it again. "You've hit some Arctic headwinds coming from Sweden and they always bring snow. You didn't think this through, did you?"
My pace dropped down to 4 miles per hour and the chilling wind cut right through my gloves. I found a small café and took shelter while the storm passed. I say storm but in reality the snow didn't even settle. Any excuse for a coffee though and I had 3 beautiful steaming cups of it.

That's what it took to stop the Morse Code of teeth chattering to stop. Once warm I decided (or rather road signs decided for me) to get off the old Glasgow road to head north towards Lanark.

By now I was so close I just wanted to get there. I did however need to buy better gloves. Mine were just not up to the Arctic headwinds. I found some cheap ones in a roadside car shop and was off again. Wow. Warm hands. Life's simple pleasures.

Head down and into the wind I rode, with all my strength. Get me out the cold and into the pub is all I could think of. Craig manages a pub, which was rather convenient too. He's already lined me up some haggis for dinner. I've never had it before and keen to try it.

His favourite joke with gullible tourists (those two Americans from Windermere would be prime targets) is how every night he goes into the Highlands to catch a herd of haggis. He says it's surprising how many people believe that. I shouldn't really laugh because I'm not exactly sure what's in haggis myself. I know there is something to do with intestines or something. Ah well. What doesn't kill you makes you stronger.

I arrived at Lanark at around 2 pm. Craig had given me pretty good directions and I managed to find his pub in no time. I'm not sure I would have coped with getting lost. Craig was, like most normal people, at work so I parked up and made my way in. He was midway through serving a customer when he saw me. Man that boy hasn't changed a bit, except for a crazy half Scottish, half South African accent.

"Ya, man. How you's pal? I cannae believe you've cycled here bro." With that and as if by magic a pint appeared in my hand. "Come on my boy, you need this."

"Cheers mate. Damn it's good to see you fella. I too can't believe I've cycled here, which makes it even more useless that we never see each other."

"Yeah man. Drink up."

It's not long before I have another beer in hand and staring into a bowl of intestines. We are both right back in junior school mode, talking about all the things we used to get up too. Within a few minutes Craig's Scottish accent has given way to South African. That's my boy. You can take the kid out of Africa.

There was a lot of soppy nostalgia going on, but it was great to share my adventure with a very old friend. The haggis was incredible too. Most food is incredible when you cycle all day but this really was. I don't know what all the fuss is about. I'm still not sure what's inside it, and too scared to ask, but I loved it.

"Remember that time we got smashed on sherry on the farm."

Craig is referring to the first time we got properly smashed together. We went and stayed on their farm for the weekend. His parents farmed day old chicks and sold them on to other farmers who didn't fancy dealing with the hatching and incubating side of things. Business was good and their incredible farm showcased their successful business. His parents were pretty easy going and when we arrived we were handed a quad bike, 2 shotguns, a kayak, an off road car, a few beers and some sherry and told to go have fun. They only had one rule: Put the guns away as soon as you have a drink. Owning guns was just part of the growing up experience in Africa. We all knew everything there was to know about shooting and hunting. I could even dissemble a 9mm pistol in less than 20 seconds. A skill that every 9 year old should know. Kidding! Guns are bad!

Anyway, we didn't actually do any shooting that weekend. We went quad biking, canoeing and had a barbecue, or braai as it's known in South Africa, in the evening. This is when the sherry came out. That's all I can remember. Apparently I confessed my love for a girl we went to school with, decided I wanted to swim naked and then passed out at 10pm. I woke up with the biggest headache the world has ever seen and vowed from that day on to never drink again. A vow I have *obviously* kept to this day.

The rest of the night (we're back in the present day now by the way) was spent reminiscing, and much like that time on the farm I didn't remember much after a few beers, some whisky and my haggis.

Craig in Lanark

Lanark

My head hurts. What happened? Why am I not on a chicken farm? I wake up in the spare bedroom and make my way to the living room to find about a million empty beer cans, half a bottle of whisky and the remains of some haggis on the coffee table. Must have been a good night. Do Scottish people have haggis when they are drunk like we have kebabs? I hope so! I've decided to take the day off. It'd be rude to come all this way and not spend a day with Craig.

After trying to clean up the flat, and giving up, we went and hit some golf balls (badly) at the driving range. I'm no golfer but it's always a good feeling smashing the hell out of that little white ball. The trick is not to look where it goes. That's when you get depressed. The fun is in the sound and the connection. If you concentrate on that – as a non-golfer – then you'll have a great day at the driving range. I don't even want to know how many balls I lost.

The driving range was followed by a game of tenpin with some of Craig's pals. I was awesome. No I wasn't. I was worse at bowling than golf, but at least I couldn't lose the balls. I eventually resorted to throwing the thing with my left hand to see if that made a difference. It didn't. It was obviously even worse and very nearly did lose a ball. Now I know why they have wire cages around the TV screens above each lane. What was I thinking?

We still had a laugh though and the beers kept rolling. Craig also didn't let me pay for a thing. Cheeky bugger. We spent the rest of the day chilling, eating, drinking and talking about old times. It's exactly what I needed.

Shanking another golf ball

Craig taking the piss at how bad I was

Lanark to Callander

I really didn't feel like getting back on the bike today. Not because I don't want to cycle, I really do, and can't wait to see the rest of Scotland. I just don't see Craig enough and wanted to spend another few days with him. Unfortunately he has a real job and has to work, so it made sense for me to push on. I also knew that the next 20 miles or so would be navigating through Glasgow and we know how much I hate cities. I was close enough already not to worry about landing up in the centre at nightfall, which would apparently result in my death according to quite a few people.

"You dunnae wan to be goin ther at night like. Ther a dodgy peple like. Gangs an stuff like," said the drunken homeless man sitting by the ATM. If he thinks it's bad then it must be bad.

Apart from having to avoid being killed in Glasgow I still had a good few hours of traffic lights, trucks, and roads without a hard shoulder to look forward too.

Naturally I had a few cups of coffee before saying a quick goodbye. I hate goodbyes. On the rare occasion when I'm not the last one standing at a party (I'll let you choose to believe that or not) I'll often just disappear instead of saying goodbye. I hate that whole; everyone is looking at me, do I shake *all* their hands or give them a hug, one kiss on the cheek or two. Damn it! I've had 8 pints. I just want my bed, which is now flying around my room so fast I have to wait for the right moment to jump on it. Do you really care I am going? Also, it can be a mood killer if people start to realise

people are going home from a party. I'd rather just make a sly exit and send a text in the morning saying thank you.

So leaving Craig's was quick and simple. "Cheers mate, awesome time" – cough, cough – "Must do it again yeah. Come to London soon. Bye."

And off I rode nearly getting run over at the same time. Must get back into cycle mode quickly.

"Stop being a wimp. Are you going to cry? You think you are hard-core but deep inside you're just a little baby."

It was true. (The me being emotional bit, not the me being hard-core – I'm really not.) I felt a little emotional but at least I was excited to carry on cycling anyway.

I was right. The next few hours were awful. Navigating through the edge of Glasgow without a map while having to stop every mile for a traffic light made for pretty slow progress. At least the weather was good and I knew I'd be in the Highlands soon. Whenever I read the words 'Highlands' on the map I think of that movie; The Highlander where the guy was immortal. I'd love to be immortal! Mainly because I love all things old. My most searched words on eBay are simply rustic or vintage. I often just search those keywords to see what comes up. I'm like a kid in a candy store when it comes to old things and don't even let me near a charity shop after payday. I'm pretty sure Oxfam's shares double in value whenever I go into one of their shops.

By midday I was out of The Glasgow Death Zone and heading for the William Wallace Monument. It had to be done and seeing as I saw the town that used his face paint to colour their doors, it'd be rude not to.

I was making good miles. The rest day certainly helped

my tired legs recover. I was powering up them hills. I arrived at the monument and saw a massive statue of William Wallace. Actually. It's blatantly a statue of Mel Gibson. It looked exactly the same. This whole area looked about as old as the film was. I wouldn't be surprised if the film put this place on the map. Parts of it were tacky touristic spin-offs on the movie, but if you looked past all that Chinese made tatt, and read up on the actual story then it was quite amazing. I don't know much about that time in history and would never have come here if it weren't for the film. I don't pretend to be a history buff and although parts of it were commercialised, I am still thankful that the film brought me here and gave me an insight into his life. Also my father looks a bit like Mel Gibson and I wanted to send him a photo.

Heading further north and onto the Highlands is incredible. Cycling along the lochs, flanked by snow-capped mountains makes me think about Mr Wallace and his army making their way through the valleys on horseback. It must have been incredibly hard to live in these cold harsh climates back then. I'm cold now and it's not even proper winter and I'm wearing 21st century, top of the range winter cycle gear. Back then they wore a skirt and a dear skin. Hard-core!

My route takes me even further north towards Callandar. The air is brisk but at least it's sunny. I faffed a lot at the Wallace Monument so it's not long before I decide to camp up for the night. I have a feeling it's going to be cold tonight but seeing as I have a -15 sleeping bag, I'm sure I'll be fine. It's more the getting out of the bag in the morning that I have trouble with.

It stays a lot lighter for a lot longer up here. I set up my tent in yet another practically empty campsite and head to the local Inn for some haggis and a pint. I don't feel tired at all today. I didn't do that much mileage and stopped loads all day. Damn traffic lights. The sky is still pitch black with piercing stars. I'll never get sick of them. I can't look up for too long though as my neck hurts. Really need to do more stretching. I say more. I need to *start* stretching. I haven't done any all trip. Naughty me!

I wrap up in my tent, and realise how quiet it is. Nothing is out tonight. All the badgers, robins and squirrels are also wrapped up nicely somewhere ready for a chilly night. I read a few pages of my book and before I know it am fast asleep. Book on chest, like an old man.

Freeeeeddddoooooommmm!!!!!!!

William Wallace

Callander to Glencoe

It rained again last night but not too badly. Must have been one of those small quick showers. I didn't even wake up in the night so it must have been quick. You know what rain can sound like on a tent. My clothes and towel are still wet so I skip my morning shower. (That made sense at the time.) I have a quick bowl of cereal and am ready to go by 8 am.

There aren't too many roads in this part of Scotland so have to stick to the main road heading northwest. They aren't too busy but every now and then I have to grizzly bear up for some heavy draught wind from oncoming trucks.

There is also a surprisingly high amount of road kill. Hopefully the money I raise for charity will help protect these little, and sometimes big, fellas. You'd have thought the animal kingdom would have learned that dark hard road + loud noises + bright lights = potential death!

By midmorning I was starving again and stopped for another breakfast. I chain Valerie up and walk into a hippy looking café. The first thing I notice was the waitress. She was stunning and around my age. Athletic build, long dark hair and she had a retro style to her. I fell in love with her straight away.

"Good morning Sir, what can I get you today?"

Oh, and she had the best accent in the world. I'm in love!

"Um, hel. . .um, hello, yes, um, please can I have a fry-up

of some sorts. . . please. Sorry!"
Why did I say sorry? I wasn't sorry, except for being a complete fumbling idiot. I could barely look her in the eyes. God I'm useless. I'm worse than Hugh Grant in any one of his films. Where's Little Flying Cow when you need him.
"Oh, I'm sorry Sir, we don't do fry-ups but we can sort you out with some oatmeal toast, green tea and some muesli if you'd like."
Seriously, what café doesn't do fry-ups but I didn't care. I'll take anything. She's lucky she is pretty otherwise I'd be off like a Jewish foreskin.
"Yes please, that would be great. Thank you."
With that she smiled, gave a flick of her hair and was off into the kitchen.
"You're such a loser. Man up and talk to her."
Little Flying Cow was right. Why wasn't my magical cycle clothing adventure façade working today? Next time she comes back I'll start a proper conversation that doesn't begin with, erm, or um, or ahhh! I mutter to myself knowing full well the odds were against me.
A few minutes later she brought me my tea. I was just about to make conversation and say something intelligent when she said.
"I see you are cycling. If you are going north then you have to follow the cycle path. It's amazing and follows the old railway line. It's much better than the road and starts just a wee way up on the left."
"Oh, OK. Thanks!"
She was already halfway back to the kitchen before I could even finish my sentence. Please come back. I said to myself trying to not sound desperate for companionship that wasn't

made of Aluminium.

She never came back. Someone else brought me my food. The chef I think. He was literally the most opposite a human being could physically be from the hot waitress. If Carlsberg made disappointment!

That's probably a good thing because I would have probably said something daft anyway. It's better to quit while you're ahead right? She had given me a hopefully good route to cycle and I was excited to see it. I gobbled my food down in haste to start my new mini adventure. I said goodbye and thank you to an empty room and heard the pretty waitress shout goodbye back from the kitchen. I wondered if I'd ever see her again. Probably not but I didn't care now that I had something else on my mind – the train track cycle path.

The entrance to the cycle path was well signposted and after a very sharp zigzag climb I was eventually on the old train track. It was incredible. A proper paved mini road that I had all to myself. I cycled along, passing through old stone railway bridges overlooking the valley to my right and the snow-capped mountains high above. I could feel the sense of adventure getting stronger.

The path didn't last that long and I was soon back on the road again. It didn't seem right to be here. I wanted more off road paths. I took my map out to investigate. At first I saw nothing but the main road heading north, but then, about 5 miles ahead I saw a thin dotted line saying "West Highland Way". Yes please. Even the name sounded epic.

I raced ahead as I wanted to get there as quick as

possible. Before I knew it I was at the beginning of what looked to be a really old stone path. Like the ones you see in old Roman Empire films. Perfect. My mind was already back in time, reliving what it must have been like all those years ago. Knights in shining armour, taking Arthur in a horse drawn carriage into the Highlands to stay in one of his many castles. They had adventures every single day. I loved the idea of that. I too am now going to follow in the footsteps of thousands of people, horses, kings, cows, and more.

"FREEEEEEDDDDDDDDDDOOOMMMMMM."

Damn you Braveheart! That's all I'm going to hear from Little Flying Cow over the next few days.

The track was pretty bumpy but loved it. My tent fell off Valerie once or twice due to the vibrations but that all added to the adventure. I was conquering this ancient road and loving it. I had to navigate my way over boulders and through mud patches. I was having a proper adventure. Have I said the word 'adventure' enough? This was an adventure in case you didn't know.

After the initial bumpy climb the road flattened out to a smoother gravel section. The scenery was, as always, breath-taking. I felt alone but not lonely. The going was slow, but that was partly because I wanted this section to last longer. I would cycle for a bit then have to get off Valerie and push her over some rocks, back on for a few hundred metres and then off the path again to avoid a big mud patch.

I tried to cycle through one of the mud patches but my semi road tyres cut through them like butter. I was slightly worried about my spokes breaking so took extra care on the rocky bits. A few times I even had to lift Valerie down a 2 foot drop. Damn she was heavy. It took me over two hours to do 8 miles and I was really sad to be back on the main road again. It just didn't satisfy the adventurous side of me as much.

I pushed on for a few more miles until I reached the top of the Glencoe Pass. What lay before me got me straight out of my post off-road blues. I hadn't realised just how high I had climbed over the last few days. Below me lay the best downhill I have been on in my entire cycling career – a whole 3 weeks long. (My cycling career that is. You can't get a hill 3 weeks long although can you imagine!) Words can't describe the feeling of freewheeling for what seemed an eternity as the brisk air rushed past my ears. I felt like a bird. All coldness, pain, hunger and discomfort melted away. Overhanging rocks zoomed a few feet past my head as I cut the corners. I must have been going 100mph. Surely!

Annoyingly, and this goes for all downhills, they are never long enough. 2 days of climbing for 15 minutes of downhill. Worth it? Hell yes!

I was only 15 miles from Fort William but decided to camp up at the bottom of Glencoe. It was very quiet and I managed to find a campsite near one of the many lochs. It was very windy and this time avoided having to chase my tent across the field. I set up camp behind one of the stone walls. 10 out of 10 for tent placement.

Because of my off-road adventures, I hadn't managed to buy packet pasta to cook so went to the only place I could find which happened to be a slightly posh restaurant. At this point I'd have given my little toe for a bowl of soup. When you are that hungry you lose all reasonable thought process.

Luckily I had managed a shower and changed into my jeans which I have just realised haven't been washed for probably 6 months. I never wear this pair at home, which is why I brought them with me. It didn't matter if I trashed them. They sit in my cupboard along with other various bits of oversized clothing I bought in the 90's or were given for Christmas. Never the less the posh restaurant let me in and I ordered Scottish Bangers and Mash and half a bottle of wine. Well not half a bottle, that can't be done. I had two large glasses. Hopefully the wine will help me sleep through the gale force wind outside.

1 am – I can't sleep. It's so windy that one of my tent pegs even got pulled from the earth. Either that or an angry mole was getting rid of the new addition to his bedroom. I'd like to think Mrs Mole did a little dance on it first. In all seriousness though, one of my tent poles is surely going to break soon.

The old train track

West Highland Way

Glencoe to Fort William

Bloody wind kept me up all night but my tent survived. I feel like death. Luckily it's not far to Fort William. I've decided to climb Ben Nevis, which I'm really looking forward to. I pack up my tent and change direction, heading northeast. The road follows a loch, which looks bitterly cold and I reach Fort William by brunch. It's a beautiful day and not a cloud in the sky, which makes for perfect conditions to climb a mountain. I had enough time to do it today but needed some more information, maps, and route options so went to the information centre.

"Good morning, I am looking for some info and maps on climbing that hill over there," as I pointed up at Ben Nevis.

"It's not just a hill pal, people die up there."

Not quite the response I thought I'd get.

"Um, sorry, I'm sure. What's the best route to go up on?"

"You mean you've never done it before, and you are on your own?"

"Just me. My first time up here. I can't wait," still sounding excited.

"Oooh, It's very dangerous this time of year. All the snow has frozen and it's very icy up there. Do you have an axe, crampons and proper boots?"

I looked down at my tatty trainers.

"No, I don't have any of that. Can I rent some?"

"Yes but if you've never used them before I suggest you

give it a skip this time pal."

"What the???? We're in our mid twenties, quite fit, and fairly athletic. We've conquered almost this entire island enduring every element thrown at us. This is just a bloody hill. Come on people. Don't throw your health and safety shite at us. We're not Pink Ties!" Little Flying Cow was angry.

"Mmmm, OK."

I turned away without trying to disguise my annoyance. This guy made it sound like Everest.

By now it was nearly midday and I decided to sleep on the idea. I found a campsite, set up my tent and started to chat to other people thinking about climbing. Most were pretty worried too. They obviously got the same speech from Captain Info. I can be quite stubborn when it comes to achieving things. My mind is often a lot stronger than my body and I tend to say yes to everything. The idea of not being able to do something that involved physical activity was not in my vocabulary. Surely it can't be that bad.

I chatted to a few more people about my concerns and most were slightly concerned too but one or two said I'd be fine and shouldn't listen to the 'health and safety crowd'.

"You will be fine pal. Don't listen to that fat bastard in the hut. He's probably never been up there," said one fairly drunk guy outside a pub. I admired his nonchalant attitude, albeit very Ale induced.

After a few more chats with people, I decided to go for it. If it got too bad then I could always turn back. I figured I should get the gear Captain Info suggested so went to the hire shop and sorted myself a nice pair of boots, crampons and an axe. I felt like a real adventurer walking back to my tent even though I managed to put a small hole in my jeans with one of the crampon spikes. They weren't even on my feet yet. I had no idea how to even fit the bloody things either so spent a good half an hour adjusting the straps for a good fit while putting loads of small holes in the campsites lawn.

I must look like such a rookie. Mountain Rescue: Get ready. Tomorrow, I'd wake up early and hit the hill, I mean mountain, hard.

The beautiful highlands

Getting ready for Ben Nevis

Ben Nevis

My alarm woke me up at around 6 am and I was on my way by 7 am. It was a beautiful day and there were already hundreds of people on the mountain. I may have had top of the range boots, crampons and axe, but I was still wearing £10 jeans, a cycle jacket and cheap service station gloves. I didn't care. I was on another new mini adventure.

Most of the climb (actually all of it) follows a path made up of big stones. This made it a lot easier to climb with my big heavy solid soled boots. By now my legs were pretty strong and I seemed to be overtaking people every minute. This became a little game. Overtaking an old couple: 2 points. A young couple: 4 points. Someone in a red jacket: 6 points. Someone else with crampons: 8 points. A ginger person: 10 points. Up and up I climbed, getting points, chatting with people I passed and stopping once to fill up my bottle with river water. I hadn't done that since Dartmoor. I love the slight mossy taste of it.

By the time I reached the snow, I was pretty much alone and had racked up a whopping 196 points. So close to my double century. I was excited at the prospect of using crampons for the first time. I put them on and started up the snow. The path was completely covered by snow and because I seemed to be the first person up, I could make my own route. That excited me. I had crampons and an axe and was definitely going to use them.

I found a few steep bits and worked my way up, digging my feet in deep and throwing the axe hard into the icy snow above. The sound and feel of metal going into the hard ice excited me even more. Step by step, grab by grab, I headed straight up. No zigzagging for me. Sir Ranulph, eat your heart out. My little solo adventure was getting better and better, my nerves from yesterday were now complete excitement. There was still not a cloud in the sky. Perfect conditions.

It was then that I heard a shout below me. I dismissed it as some kids having fun and continued carving my own adventure up the mountain. About 10 minutes went by and then I heard it - the shudder of a helicopter. I could see it in the distance, all bright and yellow as it made its way straight for me.

Normally the sound of a chopper excites me but this time I knew it was for something serious. I sat down, my heart beating fast both from the climb and the anxiety. I waited and watched as the chopper got closer, and louder. Eventually it stopped and hovered about 100 feet below me.

A paramedic was hoisted down to below my line of sight and then 5 minutes later came back up with a teenager. The efficiency was incredible and before I knew it they were off again and I was alone on what seemed a much quieter mountain.

"You should probably tell someone you are here, mate."

He was right. I should. I'll call my friend Jenny just in case. I took my cheap gloves off and hung them on my axe which I had pegged into the snow. It wasn't cold at all. At least I had reception and gave Jenny a call.

"Jenny, how's it going?"

"Not bad. You still on your bike then?"

"Yes, just on Ben Nevis and seen someone get rescued by helicopter. It's quite icy."

"Yeah, but you'll be fine. I know you. You can do anything Seanie."

I hate that nickname. There are a few friends that call me that, all girls of course. I liked her confidence in me, albeit totally unjustified.

"Thanks, but just in case, if I don't call you by 4 pm then I've fallen off the edge so can you call emergency services please."

I was trying to make light of the situation so as not to stress her out. It's a fine balance between being just serious enough for her to actually do something about it and just light-hearted enough so as not too stress her out all day.

"Sure Seanie. What's the number?"

Oh God! I've chosen the wrong person haven't I?

"999."

"Oh yeah, ha-ha."

I'm going to die a slow lonely cold death down a crevasse aren't I?

"Right gotta . . . . "

Just then I saw something that made me feel like a complete idiot. A jogger. Seriously. This guy was jogging down the mountain in nothing but skimpy running gear. No boots, crampons, axe or anything.

"Um, you know what Jenny, I think I'll be fine. Gotta run. Catch you later."

I was annoyed. Mr Jogger Man had, in one fail swoop, totally devalued my epic mountaineering adventure. The steep bit I was climbing up became practically flat in my mind. I stood up and for the first time looked around me. I was so focused on digging & cramping (yes those are the official mountaineering terms that I totally made up) I didn't even take notice of the beautiful scenery.

Visibility was practically 100%. I could see all the snow capped mountains miles and miles all round. I felt the most isolated I've been so far this trip but it was good to still be alone up here because I knew the queue of people that were just about to make the summit would ruin it. I raced to the top so that I could spend a little longer alone to take it all in. I found the emergency hut but there was so much snow you could only just make out the roof. It normally stands 15ft in the air.

I had a good 10 minutes by myself before 2 lads came up from the other direction. They couldn't have been more than 20 years old. 17 or 18 I am guessing. They seemed to have all the standard gear you need for hiking but the thing that made them stand out was the huge coil of climbing rope they had around their necks. Wow. Where have they been climbing? I've never done north face climbing.

"Hey guys. Where have you come from? Can you do proper climbing that side?"

I sounded like such a tourist.

"Yeah pal, we hammocked up on the north face last night."

"You did what?"

"Yeah, we drilled into the ice and slept on the cliff. It was cold mind!"

They slept on the ice cliff. It took a while to actually realise what that involved. These two guys were my new heroes. That sounded epic. I've seen photos of people who do that but never met anyone, and they were so young too. Good on them.

"So what do your folks think about it?"

"Um, they don't know. We told them we were going to the beach for a few days."

That's awesome. I love it. We chatted for a little longer as I quizzed them on anything and everything concerned with ice climbing. During this time the summit got more and more crowded as flocks swarmed up the tourist track.

You can only sit in one place for so long when it's this cold. My £10 jeans were practically freezing to my arse so I said my goodbyes and headed down the mountain. The crowds were on full force coming up, slipping and sliding all over the shop. It was quite funny to watch but everyone was in good spirits. Having crampons, although not *needed*, certainly made things a lot easier.

I met a group on the way down that I'd seen yesterday. They were one of the nervous groups. They all had crampons except one fella. I didn't really need mine anymore and gave him mine as long as he promised to hand them back to the hire people. If he didn't then I would have to open a can of whip-ass, and then close it again because, honestly, I'll never see him again. I'd just have to risk it. They seemed a pretty trustworthy bunch anyway.

Coming down is always worse than going up. My knees were killing and I started to get blisters. I wasn't thinking about that though. I had just conquered Ben Nevis in the snow, seen some people getting rescued and met some crazy ice climbers. What a great day adventuring. Turns out 7 people were taken off the mountain by chopper today so I guess Captain Info was probably right. He had to try and dissuade people otherwise you'd get more idiots like me, but with bigger bellies, thinking it's an easy climb, which it's not.

By early evening I felt quite stiff. Mainly in my arms. I had used a whole new set of muscles, which I hadn't used in a while. I liked it. It made me feel like I had done something really tough. That thought was always short-lived because Little Flying Cow would remind me of Mr Jogger Man:
"Ha-ha. You're an idiot. Look at that guy. He didn't use all that gear you paid money for and was going much faster than you."
Damn you Mr Jogger Man, but I applaud your skill and seemingly effortless speed as you gracefully floated down the mountain. Damn you!

Just before bed, which was embarrassingly early – 9 pm I think, I got a call from the group I lent my crampons to. They had made it and I could hear the buzzing in their voices. They returned the gear and invited me out for a few drinks.

Normally I'd have jumped at the occasion but for some reason felt like a quiet night in. Not even I understood my thought process. I'd spent 3 weeks alone and finally when I get the opportunity to go out and have a good time I say no! Has all this 'alone time' turned me into a hermit? I hope not. Eventually I fell asleep happy with the day's activities.

Watching some kids getting rescued

On the top of Ben Nevis

Fort William to Loch Ness

The sun gets my arse out of bed at 7 am. It's bright. I love Scotland. It's been a lot drier here than I expected. Maybe it's just that summer is coming – slowly.

There aren't too many people about this early except for a bunch already heading up Ben Nevis. Breakfast consists of some cereal. I've bought the mini kids variety packs and put the milk straight onto the bag. I have two of them. Frosties and Coco Pops. It's not a 3-2-1 fry-up but I can eat it in my sleeping bag and that makes it cooler.

I leave Fort William and head for the canal path towards Loch Ness. It's very spooky. The water is almost pitch black.

"We could totally swim in there. Come on. It'll be awesome."

I wasn't so sure. I'm not sure even fish live in there. I was wrong. They do, but still, it didn't look too inviting and it was still quite cold.

Cycling along the slightly gravelled path gave me a new game. Every now and then a stone would get caught in my tyre tread and then get flung into the back of my mudguard. It would then bounce up and down between the guard and the tyre, making a sound like a machine gun before shooting out the front of the mudguard. This amused me.

I became a soldier and every time I heard the gunfire I

was ready and aiming at something on the road to shoot at. I didn't have much time though, because each stone was only bouncing around for about 1 second. I wasn't very good. Firstly because in order to aim for something, you need to be cycling straight towards it (you can see the problem there) and secondly my range was only a metre at the most. I never did hit any targets and eventually became comfortable with the fact I'd be a crap soldier and should never join the army.

I got bored of the canal path so decided to do some off-road forest cycling. The huge trees were shading the moss-covered ground. Birds chirping away in the canopies and the occasional squirrel scurrying up a slippery trunk as soon as he saw me. I love forests. The smell, the sounds, the atmosphere; it reminded me of a book I read when I was a kid. My Side of The Mountain; where Sam Gribley ran away from New York City to go live in the Catskill Mountains. He made his home inside a huge tree and had a Falcon as a pet.

I pictured myself doing that one day. Living off the land, in a tree. No, actually, not a tree, a small stone cottage. Like the ones I saw in the Lakes. I've gone over this already.

At least this route was keeping me off the busy A82 road, which is pretty much the only road heading up along the lochs. Having the status of only road in the area brings with it hundreds of huge tour busses bringing more excitable Americans in search of The Loch Ness Monster.

Although I wasn't on a bus, and also not American, I too was excited about reaching Loch Ness. Everyone has preconceived ideas of what it will be like and when it first appeared in the distance I was surprised at just how big it was. In my mind it was just a small landlocked loch (say that quickly 10 times) surrounded by willow trees with the occasional swan floating along. It was in fact practically an ocean. There were ships on it. It was gi-huge-ous. Does it have tides? Must look that up. (Never did and still don't know the answer.)

Meandering along the shoreline made me think about the monster that lies within its depths. We all know the story but there is always the question, What if? I had another book when I grew up called: When Hippo Was Hairy and it told creatively made-up tales of African animals and how they came to be. Reason as to 'How The Zebra Got His Stripes' sees Zebra and Baboon having an argument. Baboon was guarding his waterhole as dazzling white Zebra came to drink without asking. After a brawl in which Baboon was kicked into the rocks, Zebra lost his balance and fell into Baboon's campfire, charring his perfectly white coat into a stripy pattern. Stories like this fuelled my young creative mind as I hope Nessie will fuel the minds of many young children all over the world.

At the top end of Loch Ness was the biggest lock I have ever seen. Is that right? You get 'locks' on 'lochs'? I'm sure you know what I mean. Anyway, there were a series of them that were so big you could fit huge cruise liners in them.

It was amazing seeing something the size of Wales (cheap dig, sorry Wales. I should have gone with whales) being lifted up. It was funny seeing tourists photographing tourists. The tourists on the ship were photographing all the tourists on the edge of the lock who were in turn photographing all the tourists on the ship photographing them back, and so on. One German couple even bought me a pie which was kind of them.

After a hour or so and one too many people with binoculars saying, "I saw him, honestly, there was a splash." I decided to head north so as to avoid Inverness. The wind started to pick up a bit. A cold northerly keeps my pace well below 10mph.

Eventually at around 5 pm I find another campsite and it's overflowing with people. Um! No. It's empty. Again! Never mind! I'm so used to my own company now anyway. I think I might change my middle name to Hermit.

The campsite has a few really old vintage tractors in the field and we know how much I like old things. I pick a spot to set up camp right next to the oldest one. I think it's an old Ford but can't be sure because it's falling apart. I always love the metal bum-moulded seats these old tractors have. I look around to see if anyone is looking and jump on it and pretend I'm racing across the Highlands.

"Freeeeeedddddooooommmmmmm!!!!!"

To be fair, that's exactly what I felt like. The wind still so strong if I closed my eyes I actually thought I was flying along. I was just getting into the swing of it when I saw a man walking up the driveway to the campsite. He had a huge backpack on. I jumped off the tractor suddenly feeling like a bit of a tit. He hadn't seen me though. His head held low and his pace slow but eventually he made his way up to where I was starting to put up my tent.

"Hello mate," he said, sounding very tired.

"Hey mate. Damn that's a lot to carry. Hope you haven't come far?"

"Ha-ha. Well, I'm kind of walking the length of Britain."
No way. What a hero. I had just cycled it and thought that was tough. I couldn't imagine walking it. He was even more mad then the ice climbing guys from yesterday.
"Wow, I'm cycling it and I thought that was hard. Tell me you are near the end?"
"Nope, just getting started. It's taken me a week to get from John O'Groats to here."
That's crazy. I only had a few days to go. He had a few months to go. Three as it turned out.
"James by the way, nice to meet you."
"Sean; you're an idiot."
We both laughed. I'm certain he gets that a lot.

After putting up our tents there was that awkward moment when we both emerged from our own tents and stood there in silence as if waiting for the other to make the first move, so to speak. Eventually James mentioned he saw a pub up the road. Perfect. I'd love to pick his brain a bit more. So off we walked, hand in hand (kidding that didn't happen) to have some food and a few beers. James was about my height and age and turns out he lives a few miles from me in London. Such a small world filled with small people on big adventures.

We sit and chat for ages about why we are doing these adventures, the good parts and the bad parts. Within minutes of hearing about James' first week, I realise that walking is tough. If I want food, it's easy for me to pop a few miles down the road to a supermarket, but for him that could be a 2 hour detour.

Also walking on the main roads is pretty dangerous and he retold a few sketchy moments when he had to jump into the hedgerow. The one similarity we both encounter was the fact we both got songs stuck in our head whenever a car drove by playing loud music.

By 11 pm and four pints later, we agree it's probably bedtime and walk back to the tents in the dark. I was in two minds about his adventure. It was certainly a lot harder than mine and would probably be more fulfilling on completion, but *walking*, mainly along the main roads is just so dull. Good on him for doing it though. Tough guy!

It was nearly midnight by the time I fell asleep which was a lot later than normal. I hope I am not too tired in the morning.

The back roads are much more scenic

An awesome old tractor – that is all

Loch Ness to Tain

Although I went to bed later last night I'm still up at 7 am. Body clocks are amazing aren't they? I have two more cereal packets and a cup of tea in my tent. James seems to be awake too and I emerge to see him packing up.
"Early start for you too then?" I ask.
"Yup."
He seemed quite tired too.
I have had way more experience in packing and unpacking and can see he still hasn't quite worked out the system yet. Not bad though. It's harder with a rucksack.
We part ways and wish each other a quick good luck. It's clear he doesn't like lengthy goodbyes either. I still don't envy him though. That's a long, long way to walk.
(James went on to finish his epic walk and raised loads of money for charity. Well done, you crazy man.)

I decided to keep slightly west on the 'B' roads to skip Inverness. Would rather be in the countryside anyway. I am also a few days ahead of schedule for some reason. My train back to London is nearly a week away and I will probably get to John O'Groats in two or three days.
"Why are you thinking about going back anyway? Come on man. We still got loads to do on this adventure. Man up and get pedalling."
He was right. I needed to stop thinking about it. It kind of

depressed me. I was enjoying this mini adventure so much and I really didn't want it to end.

The 'B' road may have been more scenic but it also had the mother of all hills. The last time I saw a hill like this was in Devon. I dropped down a few gears, put my head low and kept on going.

"Don't stop man. You can do it. All the way to the top. Go. Go. Go!!!"

Little Flying Cow was egging me on. His determination was helpful and before I knew it I was overlooking yet another great downhill into the incredible Scottish Highlands. I sat at the top of the hill and for the first time I felt in control of my body.

Looking back on the Devon days, I really didn't have a clue. I was over-pacing, under eating and having to catch my heart as it bounced out my chest on every hill. This time I felt more at ease. Yes my heart rate was still fast but it felt strong. Each chest-heaving beat felt more important and more alive as my muscles re-oxygenated themselves. I used to do a lot of exercise as a kid and competed in various canoe marathons. That was when I was 18. I am now 26 and this is the first time I have done anything nearly as hard. There was a time when I fell asleep on a night bus and had a 2-hour walk home at 4 am. That was quite hard too.

Feeling strangely proud of my ride so far I whizzed down the hill and meandered gently towards Beauly for a bite to eat. I was dreading the next section. The A9 was a busy road and the only option in this part of Scotland. I wish the Romans had made an East Highland Way. Turns out they probably did. It's now the A9. At least they can take credit for choosing the best route. Not hard when you're basically following the coast.

The forested lochs from yesterday had given way to an arid sort of scrubland, which obviously receives its fair share of nature's bombardment. The high winds and cold winters have left this section pretty bare. I liked it! What I didn't like however was the headwind nature was throwing at me today and together with the busy A9 made for pretty hard cycling.

I spent a days' worth of food budget on beer with James last night so figured I'd have to have packet pasta tonight. I found a Co-op and then after 2 campsites being closed I found one near the beach. Not the best spot to shelter from the wind but I didn't have a choice. I cooked my food and finished *The Power of One*. It's quite a big book and I didn't want to carry it with me; and was certainly not going to throw it away so I took a page out my journal and wrote:

Hello there.
Please read me. I am a very good book and
when you are done please pass me on.
Thank you.

I put the note in the book and left it on a park bench. I really hope someone finds it and enjoys it as much as I did.

Apparently I'm in the town where Madonna got married. Very random place, but then again, she is a bit random.

More old stuff

Roadkill on a SLOW road marking! Irony??

Tain to Dunbeath

Wind, wind, wind. Argh. I'm so over it all. Same mini cereal packets for breakfast, only this time it's my two least favourite left. Rice Krispies and Corn Flakes. It's still a little cold out but at least that keeps my milk from going off. After breakfast, I wrap up warm and begin one of the last times I'll be packing up. That makes me sad.

It's less than 80 miles left 'til I reach John O'Groats. I think I'll do 2 short days instead of one long day. I still have 5 more days 'til my train so have time to kill. The A9 is still busy and boring which makes me think a lot about the little stone cottage I am going to live in. It'll be completely self sufficient and I've thought of every single detail.

It'll be a completely open plan cottage. I won't have bedrooms or bathrooms. Instead the entire cottage is one very large room with a mezzanine at the one end for my bed. I'll be quite close to the celling so I'll have to sleep on a futon but with a proper mattress. Not one of those futon mattresses – they aren't great.

Below the mezzanine is my bath. A very old school cast-iron bath. Because the entire cottage is open plan, I have put a Chinese screen around it. I like the fact the bath is part of the room. It adds character.

The fireplace is right in the centre of the cottage and slightly raised off the floor so that when I am old I don't have to bend down to stoke it. The chimney goes all the way

186

through the centre of the cottage and out of the roof. There is a second fireplace near the bath and above it is a tank of water, which heats up for hot water.

The cottage is decorated with various vintage pieces of furniture and I have a very old, leather topped writing desk on one corner where I do most of my writing – on a vintage typewriter of course.

My water supply comes from rainwater running off the stone roof and into a water tank. The water tastes slightly mossy, which is how I like it. I'll probably get annoyed with not having electricity so will eventually install solar and wind but for the first few years I'll have to live by firelight and candles. I'll naturally have a few sheep, a cow and some chickens. I eat what I can and swap for what I can't. Life would be simple.

I bumped into another cyclist, which was probably a good thing because I was getting way too carried away with my little fantasy cottage. Gary was his name and he was on holiday. I think he took his bike as an excuse to get away from the family because he wasn't riding it, he was pushing it up the hill.

I can imagine him telling his wife and kids he was off for a ride and then just took his bike for a walk. To be fair to him, it was a very steep hill and it's unlikely he's had three weeks practice of cycling all day. I rode beside him for a bit and I chatted about my adventure so far. It's great thinking back about my experiences and it makes it live on a little longer.

You sometimes forget the small things and it's only when people ask you questions, that you remember them. I really don't want this to end. Getting to John O'Groats means back to Stress City and real life and that is as far from my little stone cottage as I'll ever be.

Once we reached the top of the hill Gary jumped back on his bike and dropped me like a hot potato. Bastard! Wish I hadn't waited for him on the hill now. With that I decided to stop my day early in Dunbeath. I'm annoyed. I can feel myself closing down a little and shutting off to the world. The bouncy excitement I had in the first few weeks has all but gone. In a few days' time I'll be back at home and in that rat race again. I have to give it to my business partner though. He's probably aged 100 years since I've been gone and he still hasn't called me to let me know how stressful things are. I think he knew I needed the break. He's good like that.

After the best shower I've ever had, I decide to take a walk down to the beach to clear my mind and hopefully find another mini adventure to keep me busy. I sat down and started taking in the view. I've always loved the sound of the sea. There seem to be a few people around. One drunk guy decided he fancied having a chat and came up the beach towards me. I could tell from a mile off he had had a little too much to drink. His zigzag walking pattern certainly the biggest giveaway.

"Ei thir man, wan yuz doin hur fa howday."

Honestly did not understand a word he said. Seriously. I felt like an American watching Trainspotting and needing subtitles.

"Hey mate." I said politely without making eye contact. I'm not very patient with drunks, not today anyway.

"Bla bla blaaaa bla blaaaaaa."

That is honestly all I heard. Partly because I wasn't

listening, and partly because of his heavy drunken Scottish accent.

"Yeah, for sure. Totally," I replied.

He looked confused. Turns out I got the question wrong. He staggered slightly backwards as if to walk away. He wasn't walking away at all. He was just on the verge of falling over. I got up slowly and said bye. He didn't care really. Neither did I.

I walked down the beach, thinking about my adventure and then about having to go back to London. I turned around and there he was again.

"Come on man, show him what you're made of. Tell him to bugger off."

That's what I felt like doing but didn't have the heart. I also felt sorry for the guy. I just smiled and walked past him. He stopped walking, stood in one position swaying from side to side while using every inch of energy he had to change direction without falling over.

I decided I'd had enough of weird drunk man so went back to my tent and researched my route for tomorrow. That took all of 3 minutes. There is only one road. Time for some food, so I made my way to the local pub. The warm glow radiated through the small windows. I couldn't wait.

As I walked in the door my warm excitement for a beer, and steak and ale pie was slightly overshadowed. There, propping up the bar, was the drunk guy from earlier. Really? Just my luck. Right! If I work this properly then I can avoid him. A new game.

A boring game though because all I needed to do was go through the door leading to the other side of the bar. Ah well. At least I'll be safe here.

I gobbled down a burger and snuck out avoiding gobble-di-gook conversation with the drunk guy who actually seemed to be having a real conversation with someone else. I was half tempted to eavesdrop but didn't want to risk it.

The wind had died down by the time I climbed into my very cosy sleeping bag. Just as I was dozing off a fighter jet zoomed past. Wow. I love the sound of jet engines. I'm not sure why?

"Maybe since you've been away World War Three has broken out. We'll have to live out the rest of our days here in Scotland."

Little Flying Cow was coming up with scenarios that would stop me from having to go back to Stress City. Tomorrow would be the last day of our little adventure. Why was this island so small? If there was more land I'd probably have sent my business partner a resignation letter already.

Feeling rather sad I eventually fell asleep while more WW3 fighter jets flew overhead.

Flat and bare

A bit sad to be near the end

Dunbeath to John O'Groats

I went to bed a little earlier than normal last night and was up at 6 am. I was in no rush today so I take my time getting up and having a shower. This time it was definitely the best I've ever had. Honestly. Way better than all the others.

After a quick coffee I made my way towards Wick. The going was good as I finally had a tailwind. I'd totally forgotten what it feels like to go faster than 10mph. This slightly lifted my spirits as I zoomed up the cliff edged coastline.

I arrived in Wick at around 9 am. I would need to get a train from here heading back to Inverness where I'd get my connecting train to London. I still had 4 more days 'til that train, so figured I'd just relax in Inverness and figure out a legitimate reason why I couldn't go back.

I went to the station office to get train times but the office was closed. There was a note on the door saying the office was open from 10:10am to 5:14pm. Really? Who on earth came up with those opening times? At least it made me smile. I decided to go for some breakfast. My final 3-2-1 and another huge cup of coffee.

After what seemed a lifetime waiting for the ticket office to open I eventually made my way slowly north towards John O'Groats. The tailwind picked up nicely.

"This is going to be a BREEEZZZZZEEEEE..."

"Awful joke, Little Flying Cow."

"Anything to put you in a better MOOOOOOOOOOOD."
OK. That one might have made me smirk slightly. Yes, the big smog was awaiting me but I figured it's better to remember the good parts and take them with me into the smog, use them to keep me inspired and focused.

The final 17 miles took me less than an hour. I do love a good tailwind. Finally I saw it, the sign that has brought many a smile to tired and jelly-legged End to End cyclist. 'John O'Groats – A welcome at the end of the road'. I had made it.

I freewheeled slowly to where I thought 'the end' should be. It was a tiny slipway leading into the small harbour. There was no one around and the, what used to be a hotel, was boarded up. What a spooky place. A bit of a dump really.

Maybe it gets better in the summer. I put Valerie on her stand and walked to the water's edge and sat down. The ocean was very still. Not quite mirror smooth but not far off. I've always had images of rough seas pounding the coastline up here but it was far from that. A bit of an anti-climax really.

As I sat there overlooking the Scottish Ocean in an almost numb state, two more cyclists rode up. Young guys. Probably 18 or 19 years old.

"Hey chaps. Have you just done End to End?"

"Yeah man. We are knackered, but we've made it."

They hugged each other and both had the biggest smiles on their faces.

"How long has it taken you both?"

"Just under three weeks but we've done it on those stupidly

heavy mountain bikes."

I hadn't really noticed what bikes they were cycling. Shows how much of a cyclist I am. You'd have thought by now I'd be at least a little interested in actual bikes and cycling. It's weird actually. Valerie was more of a means to get around. The adventure itself had nothing to do with the cycling and everything to do with the places I camped, the food I ate, the people I met and dealing with my own thoughts. I still wouldn't have any idea on how to change a spoke or fix a broken chain. I couldn't really even advise on what bike to buy on a future ride. I just bought Valerie on eBay and didn't change a thing. Ignorance is bliss. If you don't know it's crap then it won't annoy you. Maybe it was a good thing that I didn't know all the in's and out's of cycling. That's probably the reason I've had one of the best months of my life.

"Wow, good on you guys. It must have been really hard going?"

"Yeah man. Never again."

Just then, what must have been their family, arrived in a car and the lads rushed off. That was nice. I kind of wished my family were here. It would be nice to share my stories with people I cared about and not just random strangers in the pub. I checked my phone and didn't even have any text messages. It probably would have helped if I had actually told people I was finishing today. Never mind. I'll send some texts later. I wasn't feeling jubilant anyway and getting congratulation texts would just confirm the fact that it's all over.

I sat there staring into nothingness trying to find the energy to cycle back to Wick knowing I was up against a killer headwind. Kick a horse while it's down. I stood up and as I turned around to head back, something caught my eye, off in the distance. On the horizon about a mile off shore was a ferry heading towards me.

A ferry? Where has that come from? A little bit of inquisitive excitement started to glow in my stomach. I rushed to my map and turned the page. Orkney, of course. I had heard of The Orkney Islands but never thought that A: they were so close and B: I could get there by ferry.

My mind started to wander again.

"Come on man. Let's go to Orkney. You still have a few more days. Let's keep the adventure going."

Little Flying Cow was right. Why not go to Orkney? I had the time.

"Yes, let's do it."

With that I jumped back on Valerie and raced to the ferry port. The excitement for my new mini adventure evident by a smile paralleled to a clown's painted face. I hurtled out the car park, nearly running over the two lads while shouting.

"I will not let this adventure end, I'm heading north!"

The end

London - Four Years Later

There she lay, covered in dust, two flat tyres and sporting a very rusty chain. She was looking very, very sad indeed. I was annoyed with myself. I put Valerie away after cycling Land's End to John O'Groats (Orkney) and hadn't taken her out since. It was such a great adventure and I promised myself I'd do more such adventures. Why hadn't I? Why had I given up on living my dreams?

'Life' (or the idea of what 'life' should be) took over. Years of chasing veneered dreams left my dry mouth with nothing but the bitter taste of rat droppings. (That's my best attempt at a rat race metaphor by the way.) I didn't *hate* what I did. It was *OK*. I had started a business and it paid the bills. That's all it did. I felt as if I was in autopilot mode. I rarely got excited about anything and nothing challenged me anymore. I needed to do something about it.

With that I gave Valerie a dust down, pumped up her tyres and went on my first ride in 4 years. Little did I know that this set the ball in motion for what would turn out to be the biggest challenge of my life. 8 months later I'd set off to try and become the fastest person to cycle around the world - an adventure that would change my life.

The End

Thank you to all the kind hearted people who gave me free meals, free places to camp, and generous donations for charity.

My tips for LEJOG

1. Do it in the summer.
2. Eat much more than you normally eat, even if you aren't hungry.
3. Do it with a friend. It makes it more fun.
4. Buy a mascot.
5. Give your mascot a name
6. Take loads of photos of your mascot. It makes for a great album.
7. Do it when the sun is going to be shining most of the time.
8. Research your route to avoid busy 'A' roads.
9. Don't take too many clothes. 1 set of cycle clothes. 1 pair of casual clothes and two pairs of socks and underwear. More pairs still get dirty and stink out your bag.
10. Don't do it in the winter.
11. Be flexible with route and plan. That's allows for more adventure and meeting people.
12. Think about all the gear you are taking. You really don't need as much as you think. Cut pages out of map books, camping guides etc. It all adds up.
13. Write a journal or take a voice recorder and take loads of photos and videos. No matter how epic the adventure is, you will start forgetting it.
14. Make sure you have fun.
15. Do it when it's not raining.